# The Big OE

## TALES FROM NEW ZEALAND TRAVELLERS

Nigel McCarter

## TANDEM PRESS

*To Linda, who brought me*

First published in New Zealand in 2001 by
Tandem Press
2A Rugby Road
Birkenhead, Auckland
New Zealand
www.tandempress.co.nz

Copyright © 2001 Nigel McCarter

ISBN 1 877178 83 7

Design and production by Egan-Reid Ltd.
Printed in New Zealand by Publishing Press.

# CONTENTS

## ACKNOWLEDGEMENTS

I am most grateful to the contributors for their time and their trust. I was humbled by the willingness of people to welcome me into their homes, to talk frankly and at length about their experience and then allow me to write down their memories. Thank you.

The book has been immeasurably improved by Guiseppe di Maio who translated the Italian, Uli Nieschmidt who checked the German, Sigríður Ólafsdóttir who wrote the Icelandic, and Helena and Amir Moghadassi who wrote Parsi.

# INTRODUCTION

The 'big OE' has become part of New Zealand and Australian culture. Every year, thousands of young – and some not so young – New Zealanders and Australians fly out of Auckland, Christchurch, Sydney and Brisbane, bound for their big adventure. They venture to London as computer consultants, to America as camp counsellors, or to teach English in Japan. Some go to trace their roots; to walk with the ghosts of their ancestors, whether in the UK or the Ukraine, Denmark or Dalmatia. Others travel for the sheer delight of discovering the world and because they can.

The desire to travel is not new. When he grew up in Southland in the fifties, John Smithies ('Pawning my partner for petrol') always knew he would go 'voyaging'. But widespread travel only became feasible after World War II. Before that time, voyages by sea were long and expensive and few immigrants returned to their birth land.

That began to change after 1950. Assisted passages and social promise brought thousands of new families to Australia and New Zealand. Apart from the long-established P&O line, Greek and Italian shipping companies such as Sitmar, Chandris, Flotta Lauro and Lloyd Triestino ran the 'jumbo jets' of the age. The emigrant ships provided affordable travel to Europeans seeking a new life in the Southern Hemisphere. By the mid-1950s, vessels arrived in Sydney every week and many boats called at Wellington and Auckland en route.

The emigrant ships did not return empty. An increasing number found a ready market of passengers seeking to travel in the opposite direction. In the 1950s, immigration records show that 20,000 people a year left New Zealand, intending to return. By 1966, that figure had risen to 200,000 and in 1975, only nine years later,

7

649,514 New Zealanders left the country temporarily. Although I have no estimate of the numbers of young people leaving New Zealand for their OE, it was certainly very many.

Apart from some pre-war liners like the *Strathnavar*, many of the first emigrant ships like the *Tamaroa* and the *Ruahine* were built to carry meat and dairy produce from the pastures of New Zealand to a hungry Europe. It wasn't long before the sheer scale of emigration to Australia gave shipping lines a powerful incentive to find vessels with more passenger accommodation: live meat became more profitable than frozen.

At first the companies converted wartime troop carriers like the *Rangitiki*. This ship, which had carried 2600 troops in the Mediterranean, was refitted in 1948 for 123 first class and 288 tourist class passengers. The *Fairsea* and *Fairsky* had served as aircraft carriers. Older liners like the *Dominion Monarch* were soon replaced by faster and better equipped ships; the *Neptunia* (1951) and the *Southern Cross* (1955) were built specifically to carry passengers.

Accommodation on the earlier cargo ships and converted troop transports was austere. There was not a great deal to do, apart from sitting on deck and listening to the steady thud of diesel engines. The food was adequate, but the shipboard entertainment was strictly limited.

Dedicated passenger vessels like the *Patris* or the *Achille Lauro* (1966) made more of an effort, but tourist class was hardly five star accommodation. Cabins had four or more bunks; food certainly didn't reach haute cuisine standards. One traveller on the *Angelina Lauro* reported copious quantities of pasta and little else. Standards of hygiene were sometimes dubious; when the *Guglielmo Marconi* was refitted for the Caribbean cruise trade in 1978, the vessel failed its US Health Department inspection – seven times. Passengers reported a lively insect life in the cabins, bathrooms and eating areas.

Sometimes the conditions and cultural differences between Australian and New Zealand passengers and Greek and Italian crew caused friction. There was a passenger mutiny on the *Galileo*

*Galilei* in 1976 (see 'Mutiny on the *Galileo*'). But most of the younger passengers seemed to thoroughly enjoy themselves. On board the ship there was nothing to buy but 'the booze and there was plenty of that'. Some of the contributors I spoke to remembered the voyage with rueful fondness as one long party.

The immigrant ships are now long gone – fading black and white photographs in albums and library books. From the mid 1970s, reliable aeroplanes began to provide a more expensive, less elegant, but rapid means of transport. With the end of assisted passages, ships became unprofitable and many vessels were sold for scrap or moved to other duties. By 1976, the only liner offering regular sailings between New Zealand, Australia and Europe was the *Australis*. She made her last voyage in 1977, after which she was laid up in Timaru before being transferred to the cruise trade.

How sad. A voyage to Europe by boat sounds, and often was, a romantic adventure in itself. A cursory look at the passenger lists for the vessels show very large numbers of young women amongst the travellers. On some voyages, to the delight of the young men, there was a five to one gender imbalance.

The huge increase in women travellers was part of the post-war social change. Prior to World War II, few women would have had the opportunity to leave home outside of marriage, although Ray Amer ('Fly spray and hakas') commented that he envied the way nurses could travel from job to job. Whilst young men could satisfy their taste for adventure, often with tragic results, by enlisting in the colonial army to endure the Boer War or the trenches of France, women, by and large, were confined closer to home.

After World War II, social restrictions began to lift and young women seized the opportunity to travel unchaperoned, independent and free. The travelling women of this era came from ordinary backgrounds. There were no Mary Livingstones of independent income, but New Zealand 'girls' from the farms, factories and offices of the Hutt and the Waikato. They had a yen for adventure and freedom, often in spite of the social pressures of home. One traveller told me her father was dead set against her leaving home before marriage. Her aunts sabotaged his ruling by whispering, 'Go on, you've got to go', in her ear at every opportunity, and contributing to her travel fund.

Some of the first wave of post-war travellers felt they were returning 'home', even if they were third- or fourth-generation New Zealanders. One New Zealander told me her father had always talked of Yorkshire as home even though he had never been there. She was brought up on Beatrix Potter and Enid Blyton, so she thought it perfectly natural to head for London as soon as she left college. But when she got to Piccadilly, she wondered what on earth she had come to.

Soon that attitude began to change. Few contributors who travelled in the mid-1970s said they felt they were going 'home', although many are still interested in their family tree. Thirty years later, I doubt there are many European New Zealanders who regard Europe as their motherland, albeit we recognise our origins. In that sense, perhaps the present generation of European travellers has grown up.

The motivation for travel was, and is, more complex. It doesn't seem to me that 'finding one's roots' was ever a satisfactory or complete explanation for the travel bug. Other nationalities also travel, though there is a perception that young New Zealanders and Australians are more adventurous than most. I think the incentives to travel lie closer to home.

Many New Zealand writers and social historians have commented that New Zealanders have a sense of rootlessness. It is reflected in our literature and social statistics. New Zealanders have always been willing to move between jobs and locations. We are very outward looking; we are conscious that there is a whole world outside these small islands.

Travellers didn't seem to regard an OE as a particularly difficult undertaking: 'You just went and did it.' After all, if one's immediate forebears were willing to migrate around the world for life, a voyage on a modern liner could hardly be regarded as an impediment.

No doubt sheer curiosity also played a part. There is a deep-seated need to explore; to look at the other side of the mountain. Many young people have a perception, which may be false, that they have a limited number of years before social obligations and raising a family will tie them down.

There were also huge changes in social expectation after the war, particularly for women. Young people were less inclined to accept restrictions – let alone those that would limit their experience to one set of small islands.

Finally, there was the opportunity. The New Zealand standard of living in the 1960s and 70s was high compared with other countries. It wasn't difficult to earn your fare, although many travellers worked long months in multiple jobs to do so.

Taken in combination, willingness and rootlessness, opportunity and curiosity are a heady mix. Before long it became the 'accepted thing' to go off on the 'big OE' immediately after college and before settling down.

Almost all travellers headed for Britain. There were strong cultural and practical reasons to do so; the school syllabus and the culture of New Zealand were strongly Eurocentric. History, Geography, English and the general literature provided a sense of familiarity that also acted as a powerful magnet. Until 1970 the phrase 'British Subject and New Zealand Citizen' was written on every New Zealand passport. There were also the practical reasons of language and the ability to work without a permit in the UK, whilst it wasn't that easy to get a work permit for the USA or the rest of Europe.

At first, most travellers went to London. They headed for the Overseas Club in Earls Court (Kangaroo Valley) or to New Zealand House in the Haymarket. At both places, there were bulletin boards advertising jobs and flats. One could find travelling companions, pick up mail, or simply sit and listen to a reassuringly familiar accent. There was a shop in the alley below the New Zealand High Commission where one could buy real Marmite in straight bottles you could get a knife into and Weetbix without the 'a'.

Travellers found a huge variety of jobs and live-in positions such as nannies, and pub and hotel work were popular. In between earning a living and drinking it in the warrens of Earls Court and Amsterdam, the travellers took Contiki tours round North Africa or the Magic Bus to Greece. Eventually, after two months, or two years or more, they'd set off home. They followed the Marco Polo route to India, sailed through the Caribbean, hitchhiked back via Canada and America, or drove overland to South Africa.

Every traveller needs courage and determination, often aided by copious amounts of ignorance. Inevitably they had adventures – sometimes ordinary, sometimes funny, frightening, loving, or just plain weird slices of life. The stories recounted in this book are recollections of such episodes and are as varied as the people who told them. Some stories are adventures, others descriptions of ordinary travel events. Most, but not all, of the stories have a happy ending. Travellers did sometimes get into trouble, were assaulted, robbed or experienced other nastiness, some of which is described in this volume. All the stories show some aspect of the OE that will be recognised by other travellers.

A great many of the tales revolve around differences in culture or language. These differences led us into all sorts of scrapes that were usually resolved satisfactorily. But I found the way travellers talked about cultural differences most revealing.

On the whole, people do not remember, or at least do not choose to talk about, the museums, clothing, holy places or scenery. These are the physical embodiments of cultural and geographical difference. What impressed the travellers was how people in countries all over the world have the same aspirations and how, almost always, the good side of human nature eventually comes to the fore. There is far less evil at an individual level than we often expect. This isn't unreasonable optimism. As Dave Palmer, who contributed 'Four steps on the way to Broome', put it, 'In the remotest part of Asia and the poorest mud hut, there was always a smile and welcome'. I find that enormously reassuring and hopeful.

Overseas travel was, and still is, an astonishing phenomenon that enriches New Zealand life in innumerable ways. Travellers have brought home partners (I was brought), as well as skills, experience and memories. They lived amongst different cultures and discovered a depth to their own. They witnessed wartime devastation in Europe, and dictatorship and repression in Eastern Europe and Latin America.

Shona Thompson, who contributed 'Up against the wall in Rio Cuarto', noted a marked difference in attitude between New Zealanders and Australians, and their travelling companions from North America and Europe. We tend to assume the best rather than the worst. 'She'll be right' can be slapdash, but it can also be an expression of confidence.

Here there is no threat of war and shootings, and muggings and violence are rare. For other nationalities such calamities have been all too real. That in itself is a powerful incentive to return. Perhaps this feeling is also related to the end of one life phase and the beginning of the next. Many contributors said they returned because 'this is the finest place on earth to bring up children'; 'the school system is good' and 'the air and water are free of pollution'.

And also, because New Zealand is our home. This is our place. These are our stories. We hope you enjoy them.

# THREE-SPEED CARDIGANS

*Val Wilson's (nee Cosgrove) great-grandparents emigrated from Ireland in 1859 and the whole family were 'adventurous types'. But when she first suggested she should go abroad with older friends, her mother wouldn't allow it. Then, two months before her 21st birthday in 1953, Mrs Cosgrove gave her daughter a ticket on the TAMAROA and six weeks later, Val arrived in Britain to join her friends Yvonne Franks and Shirley Rainton.*

I sailed out of Auckland the day I turned 21. I didn't know a soul on the boat, but it was full of young people. We had a wonderful trip, sitting in the sun day after day, talking with boys, chugging across the Pacific to the Panama Canal, Bilbao and Curaçao, then across the Atlantic to Southampton.

My friends met me off the boat and we all went down to Bournemouth. At first we worked in the hotel trade, but Yvonne believed that we would earn more money in the Midlands so, after two months, we travelled north and found work in a factory making millions of buttons. I have never seen so many buttons. The work wasn't exciting, but Yvonne was right. We soon saved enough to buy three brand new bikes.

They were lovely machines, quite unlike modern bicycles: BSA Ladies Sports models, with nice thick, springy saddles, Sturmey Archer three-speed gears with handlebar change and big bells. We fitted them with pannier bags and carriers, and told the shop owner we were going to explore Europe by bike.

That caused quite a stir. It just wasn't done for three girls to go off cycling around Europe. But we were Kiwis and we could do anything.

The shop owner called the local paper and we were interviewed and had our pictures taken: all quite a fuss for a little bike ride.

Before we left, we knitted ourselves cardigans with a Kiwi on one side and a map of New Zealand on the other, with 'NZ' initials. Every time we stopped in a town, we looked for small badges and either sewed or clipped them in place on our cardigans. By the end of the trip, we were covered with jingling colour.

We aimed to cycle 20 or 30 miles each day, plotting our route so that we could stay at youth hostels. These were cheap and cheerful; we slept in dormitories on hard mattresses and cooked our own food in a communal kitchen. The fees were minimal, but hostellers had to do a job in the morning, like washing up, cleaning the toilets, or scrubbing the floor.

It wasn't that long after the war and food was still rationed in Britain. The centre of Coventry and many parts of London were ruined. Although the country areas of Belgium and France looked tranquil and unaffected, when we got to Germany we saw bombed-out buildings and piles of rubble everywhere. Although we had seen newsreels of the blitz and the war in Europe on *Pathe Pictorial* (no TV in those days), it was just another picture. It wasn't real until we actually saw it.

Despite the war, everybody was really nice. The only place we couldn't go was Spain; they wouldn't let us in because we didn't have a skirt. We had only packed trousers and women weren't allowed to wear trousers in Spain. We were told that if we wanted to visit Spain, we would have to buy a skirt. So we didn't go.

After eight weeks in Europe, we were beginning to run out of money. We caught a ferry back across the English Channel and cycled up to Scotland. We found a berry-picking job near Glasgow; we were paid three pence a 'luggie', a little pail that held about two quarts. Most of the other pickers were bodgie boys from Glasgow. They walked around in their big boots with bicycle chains around their waists, earning their money for Christmas.

I don't know how they saved any. Although they were real hard-core people they were quite harmless – until they got stuck into the whisky. We went to some of their parties and were treated as an absolute novelty. They couldn't understand our accent and we couldn't understand theirs.

When the berry-picking season was over, we biked down to the West Country. We were cycling around the hills in Somerset when Yvonne fell off her bike and split her head open. It was quite a serious injury and she ended up in hospital for a couple of weeks.

While she was in hospital, Shirley and I found work on a local farm. We stayed there for some weeks, as the manor took Yvonne in to convalesce when she came out of hospital; but she was never allowed to go into the main house and eat with the lord. Oh no, she had to eat in the kitchen with the staff.

What a laugh.

*Val, Yvonne and Shirley with their bikes.*

# LIFE IN PARK LANE

*Barbara Newburgh travelled to London on the* SOUTHERN CROSS *in 1956. She stayed at the Overseas Visitors Club in Earls Court and took temping jobs around London, until she was offered a shorthand-typing job at the Dorchester Hotel.*

There were five of us in the manager's office at the Dorchester, dealing mainly with accommodation correspondence. Everything was first class: the blue letterhead embossed with royal blue, blue ribbons on the typewriters – even the telephone number was an elegant Mayfair 8888. One girl was responsible for lost property, ranging from fur coats and jewels to diaries and playing cards. Items not claimed were auctioned or sold off every six months or so.

The hotel was owned by the McAlpine family. There were nine floors, with four suites for film stars and other celebrities. I turned 20 shortly after I started to work there, and as well as being given gifts and flowers, Miss Simmons, the manager's secretary, showed me around these suites as a birthday treat. The McAlpine Suite was first on the list. Furnished in the true, understated English tradition, it also included a radio, television and cocktail cabinets nestling behind false book fronts.

The Harlequin Suite, with its underlying Eastern influence and lavish use of mirrors, was straight out of a Hollywood film set. In fact, just weeks before, Victor Mature had been a guest in this suite but was asked to leave after writing suggestive messages for the maids in soap on the bedroom mirror.

The Audley Suite was furnished in French Empire style, with the walls and doors of the single bedroom hung in French printed linen: rather overwhelming if one was in a hurry to reach the bathroom.

The Oliver Messel Suite had been named after the famous designer, and incorporated special Messel touches like the television cabinet designed as a miniature theatre. His paintings of 18th-century English gardens and, in the bedroom, his original sketches for the ballet *Sleeping Beauty*, hung from sashes of mulberry silk. This suite was Elizabeth Taylor's favourite whenever she was in London. I caught a glimpse of her one morning in the foyer, accompanied by husband number three, Mike Todd.

Johnny 'Cry Baby' Ray had been a guest at the Dorchester, but had been asked not to return as the hotel management didn't appreciate the screaming fans outside the hotel. Poor old Johnny, no wonder he cried – he had also been refused admission to one of the restaurants for not wearing a tie. But the highlight was when James Mason called 'Good morning!' to me as he was getting into his car in front of the hotel one morning. I walked on air for the rest of the day.

The hotel was run on disciplined lines. Even the staff dining rooms had their own hierarchical structure. We dined with the receptionists and housekeepers in the 'top' staff dining room.

I was paid £6.10s per week – less than my wage at home, but the meals were magnificent, and if I was going to a West End show or movie in the evenings I could have dinner as well.

Working in the Dorchester was like living in another world. It had a unique ambience which seemed to envelop its occupants, making one feel rather special. Our office was situated quite a distance from the management offices, but it was well furnished and attractive. Each aspect of the hotel management was covered by an appropriate office – manager's, bills, banqueting – or an appropriate shop – baker's, butcher's, florist and so forth. Everything was highly professional and ran very smoothly. The doorman was an imposing figure in his green and gold uniform, top hat and white gloves. He had a sixth sense as far as cabs were concerned; no one ever had to wait. Then there were the gorgeous little bellboys, their pillbox hats perched on the side of their heads, looking all of 12, but

I guess they were about 15. The receptionists glided around, anticipating the guests' every whim and ensuring utmost comfort for all. They were all male, having served a five-year apprenticeship working in the kitchens, waiting on tables, acting as valets and spending a year on the Continent in exchange with a European trainee. Then they were allowed to dress in striped trousers and tails as fully-fledged receptionists.

The restaurants were first class, with all tips going into a 'tronc' which was then shared out equally. The waiters had been specially trained, not only to give excellent service but also to deal with the odd nuisance. One person wrote to complain about his luncheon bill. It appeared that he and his companion had each had a serving of asparagus which was so expensive that the price didn't appear on the menu (something like 30s. per serving). The most expensive item was Caneton d'Aylesbury à l'Ananas (Aylesbury Duckling with Pineapple) at £3 – almost half my week's wages.

The hotel also had its own recluse. Sir John Ellerman, a shipping magnate, lived in a suite at a cost of £1000 per week and had never been seen outside since the mid-1930s. Not my way of enjoying a fortune!

One day I was told there was another New Zealand girl working in the bills office. On meeting her, I discovered she was from Levin, where my married sister lived. I mentioned that my brother-in-law worked in the Bank of New Zealand and was astonished to learn that he had arranged her traveller's cheques and told her to look out for his young sister-in-law. The world was shrinking even then.

The staff ball was held each year on the first Saturday in May. The chairman, Sir Malcolm McAlpine, gave a welcome speech and invited us to enjoy ourselves. The mirror-lined ballroom was like a movie set, and dancing in an evening dress made me feel like a film star! My partner, Kevin, also a New Zealander, danced like Fred Astaire, so the evening was perfect.

One of my daily duties was a quaint English custom. Each morning I had to take three freshly sharpened pencils into the managing director's office and replace the ones I had put there the previous day. The MD, George Ronus, was Swiss, and a delightful person, but I'll swear he never used a pencil. On New Year's Day I caused great amusement throughout the hotel by complaining to Mr Ronus, 'I thought we were supposed to be the uncivilised colonials from the other side of the world – yet not only do we get a holiday on New Year's Day but the day after as well!' Mind you, I had attended a party at the Acton Army Barracks until 3 am that morning (including dancing with a snuff-sniffing major) which may have affected my attitude.

Fortunately, my complaint didn't affect Mr Ronus's opinion of me. When the time came for me to leave, he was delighted to give a written reference stating that I was 'reliable, honest and willing, and able to get on well with everyone'. Who could ask for more?

I have often dreamed of returning to the Dorchester, but perhaps memories are better left alone. The hotel has undergone several ownership changes over the years. She also had a magnificent facelift in the early nineties, the right of every lovable old lady who needs rejuvenating from time to time.

# PISTOL PETE

Margaret Gregan never really intended to travel. But one night in 1954 she and her girlfriend, Audrey Robins, went to see an Alec Guiness film about a sea captain. It was so romantic, they decided to try a sea voyage themselves. They saved for the fare for most of 1954, working at three jobs each. Then they took the MONOWAI to Sydney and an Italian liner called the NEPTUNIA from Sydney to Naples via Melbourne, Ceylon and the Suez Canal. They hitchhiked the rest of the way to London through Italy and the Soviet-occupied Austria through Germany, Holland, Belgium, France and Spain.

They worked in the UK for six months, then sailed from Newcastle in County Durham to Bergen in Norway, to hitchhike back through Scandinavia and France.

Margaret and Audrey in Stockholm with their haversacks and travelling gear.

I have an old black-and-white photograph of Audrey and me in Stockholm. Both of us sport a 1955 hairdo, are wearing long gabardine coats that reach well below the knee as well as sensible shoes, and are carrying with us our precious haversacks. You know, the old sort of haversack – grey canvas with an external frame, very uncomfortable and not very big, so we tied our boots and sleeping bags on the outside with string. But those packs contained everything we owned so we hardly ever let them out of our sight.

We'd hitchhike from hostel to hostel; France was the worst for this type of travel, while Holland and Sweden were by far the easiest. There was a strict protocol to hitching in those days: if you arrived at a road and someone else was hitching as well, you had to go to the far end of the queue. You'd always ask politely where the driver was going, and one person always got in the front and the other in the back.

But the two of us never waited for long and we never had any trouble getting through the borders. In fact, the haversacks seemed to make things easier – remember this was before the hippy days. If you were carrying a suitcase, you always got searched. If you had a haversack, then the guards assumed you were a poor but respectable student. How times have changed – nowadays suitcases are definitely more respectable than haversacks. Perhaps there were fewer drugs in those days.

In September, we stayed at an interesting youth hostel in Stockholm. It was a three-masted iron sailing ship called the *af Chapman* – built in Cumbria in 1888 and named after a famous Swedish vice admiral, Fredrik Henrik af Chapman, who'd lived from 1721 to 1808.

After a few days, we decided to hitch to Copenhagen, so we took a tram to the outskirts of the city and put out our thumbs. We got a number of rides and soon arrived at a small town called Markaryd. It wasn't long before a big black car, a Mercedes or Volvo, drew up.

The driver was a large, blonde Nordic man with a crew-cut and well dressed. He wound down the window and said he was heading all the way to Copenhagen. It was about 150 km to the ferry at Halsingborg, so we were delighted to get a lift right through. We put our haversacks in the boot, got in and before long he was speeding along through the pine forests.

The countryside was not particularly scenic in this area and although our driver spoke English, he didn't talk much so I remember little of the journey. But after about an hour he reached across me to the passenger's side, opened the glove compartment, took out a revolver and put it in his pocket.

I was horrified. I was convinced that he was going to drive to the side of the road and murder us. Goodness, I thought, do I have my clean knickers on? (Mothers tended to drum that into their children in the fifties. 'Always wear clean knickers, dear. Just in case you get run down by a bus.')

I must have looked startled.

'It's okay,' he said, 'Customs are always awkward about this sort of thing,' and smiled reassuringly.

I wasn't reassured and edged a little closer to the door, getting ready to run in case we started to slow down in a lonely area. I turned round to see if Audrey had noticed anything, but she was fast asleep in the back. Before long, we were driving through the outskirts of Halsingborg, well on the way to the ferry.

We drove on to the ship, as we do on the Cook Strait ferries, and as we got out the driver rather brusquely told us to leave our packs in the car and go and find something to eat and drink. I tried to whisper the news about the revolver to Audrey, but she had just woken up and didn't understand.

When we were out of earshot I told Audrey what had happened and she began to worry. Should we abandon the ride? But our packs were in the boot of the car with all our worldly goods – our clothes, cameras, clean knickers – inside. What would we do without them?

Should we tell the officers on the ferry? That didn't seem to be fair, as the man had been very generous giving us the lift. The ferry journey between Sweden and Denmark is only about 30 km, and we were still undecided when all of a sudden our driver reappeared, visibly relaxed: 'Kom, time to get back in the car.'

Very meekly and without any more discussion, we followed him back to the car deck, feeling rather foolish and apprehensive. Once in the car we began to relax, until I noticed the bulge in his jacket pocket.

By this time it was getting dark and the streets were empty. He still had the pistol. Oh what fools we were! We were going to be killed and buried in the forest. We'd disappear and our mothers would never find us. There was no one to save us.

Copenhagen's ferry port was only just outside the city. No sooner were we through the gates than our driver drew the pistol from his pocket, leant across me to the passenger's seat, one hand on the wheel, and put it back in the glove compartment. He grinned. 'The youth hostel is just here. Have a good stay in Denmark.'

# FOUR STEPS ON THE WAY TO BROOME

Dave Palmer was born in central Otago. He was working in Christchurch, when he and a couple of mates from the table tennis club decided to try their luck overseas.

After six months working in the Christchurch freezing works, he had saved enough money (£120) for a fare on the SOUTHERN CROSS, a 20,000-tonne liner that plied between Australia, New Zealand and Europe via the Panama Canal. He arrived in Britain late in 1956 and worked there for two years. Starting with a DMW (Dawson Motors, Wolverhampton) motorcycle with a two-stroke 197 cc Villiers engine, Dave toured all around Scandinavia and Europe, but exchanged it for a more powerful 350 cc Matchless before starting on his overland journey home.

S.S. SOUTHERN CROSS

The SOUTHERN CROSS.

'It was an ex-army bike, very sturdy and loaded with two panniers, a box on the carrier, then more on the box, holdall on the tank and an unsprung rear wheel. It was a lovely machine; single cylinder and it hardly missed a beat on the 15-month-long trip – apart from when an argument with a Russian taxi left the bike looking as if it had been in a motocross. I rode across Persia, Afghanistan, Pakistan, India, then all the way down to Ceylon in January 1959.'

Exhausted and sick, weighing less than 45 kg, Dave needed to find a passage home. He bluffed his way on to a boat in Colombo, sailed across the Indian Ocean to Broome in Western Australia, and then continued the ride to Sydney, where he caught the HOPE RANGE bound for Wellington.

Fairly early on in the trip, I was sheltering from the rain in a derelict house in Austria. This was not long after the war, when Austria was still partially occupied by the Soviet troops, and there were a lot of old houses around. A derelict house was better than pitching a tent and then having to pack it away wet the next morning.

I was rummaging around, getting ready for the night, when I found a hole in the floorboards. Something was glinting, so I had a poke around and found a multi-shot pistol. I thought that it might come in handy and though it was a bit rusty, I soon cleaned it up. I fired a test shot and it worked, so I hid it well down in the panniers.

I never really used it but it did provide a bit of comfort. I was threatened by nomads a few times, for example, so I waved it around just to scare them off. Then I frightened the hell out of some monkeys in India just for fun. But even though I had a pistol, I was robbed several times. One night, someone sneaked in and took my helmet and goggles.

I don't know how they managed that; I always backed the bike up close to the tent and put a trip wire round it at night. But I never heard a thing: they snuck right in, emptied the panniers and made off with my helmet and goggles. I don't even know what use it would have been to them. Probably some shepherd boy out for a lark.

Bandits in Persia were a real worry, not so much for what they might do to you, but because you only had one of everything – one petrol can, one tool kit, and so on. So when something got stolen, it could be a major disaster. Still, you had to think positively, to try and anticipate problems and cope with them if they became a reality.

I kept the pistol well hidden in the bottom of the bag; Customs sometimes gave me a bit of a hard time but they never found it. I had to have visas for every country I went to. If those weren't spot on, I had to go back to the last major city, which could be days away. However, they generally let me through.

By the time I got to Ceylon, I'd developed ulcerative colitis and was feeling pretty sick. The first thing I needed to do was find a ship going the way I wanted to go. I gathered all sorts of useful information on the road and I'd found out, for one, that if a ship takes you on, they are obligated to get you home if you are ill or get into trouble with the police. What I needed was a ship going to Australia or New Zealand and the chance of a decent meal and some clean drinking water.

The port at Colombo had several long jetties with about 20 ships moored alongside – not like the big container vessels today, but small tramp steamers from all over the world with derricks and wharfies swinging goods in nets on to conveyors, in and out.

Of course the wharf areas were all chained and fenced off, so the first thing was to bribe the gateman. A few rupees and I had the bike inside and locked in a small shed. 'That's fine,' I thought. 'Step number one.'

I walked right to the end of the wharf, eyeing up all the ships, looking for an Australian or New Zealand vessel, and asking the crewmen very discreetly where they were going. Right at the end, at the very last ship, I came across a boat headed for Australia. I asked a crewman whether they needed anyone else on board: Oh yes, he said, they needed an engineer and a cook.

Well, I knew I couldn't bloody well cook, but I'd always done my own car maintenance and the like, so I was reasonably confident about being an engineer.

'That's fine,' I thought. 'Step number two.' I then went back to the gate, collected my bike and headed into town.

Now to get on board, I really had to be a registered seaman and a union member. I'd never been either, so when I arrived back in town I immediately started looking for someone to write me a reference. In those days, anybody and everybody took a bribe, and probably still do. I didn't want anyone too smart, but there were plenty of other people who could do with a dollar or two.

I soon found a character sitting in a café reading a paper. He

*Dave on his DMW motorcycle, 1957.*

didn't look well off, but I figured he could read and write, so I sat down and started up a conversation. He spoke reasonable English and I soon found out that he wasn't a lawyer or anyone special. He was a clerk in an accountant's firm.

So, after a little while, I opened my wallet, showed him a roll of rupees and asked if he'd write me a recommendation for the ships.

'What would you like me to write?' he asked, eyeing the money.

'Ah, just something to say that I can fix an engine or two.'

Well, he smiled, and I smiled, and I got out a pad and a pen and dictated a note saying that I'd worked as an engineer at a timber mill in Colombo for the last six months and that he'd be very happy to recommend me to anyone for employment. We both thought this was a bit of a laugh, and he signed the reference with a flourish. I then passed across some of the rupees and we had a cup of tea and that was that.

'That's fine,' I thought. 'Step number three.'

If you are going to work a bluff there is no point in being hesitant about it. You have to be pretty positive, confident, make the eye contact and believe it's going to work. After all, the worst that might happen was that I would be thrown off the ship, and I'd still be in the same position.

So I rode back to the port, passed some more rupees to the gateman, walked up the jetty and the gangplank as cocky as you like, and asked to see the captain. 'I believe you're going to Australia,' I said. 'Any work I can do?' As bright and brash as my lost rupees.

'Oh,' he said, 'we need a cook and an engineer.'

'That's interesting, I've just been working as engineer.'

'Oh,' he said, 'have you indeed?'

I then pulled out my crumpled note and passed it to him. Once he'd read it, he said, 'That looks okay, we'll take you on. You can be the sixth engineer.'

With an invitation like that I soon had my bike over, into the nets and on board the deck. Step number four.

Well, they were supposed to leave the following day, but they ran into problems and we were delayed for a week. That was just great for me – I was supposed to be the sixth engineer but they didn't give me any work. Instead I lived on board with a roof over my head, some decent food and a few days up my sleeve to look around Colombo.

The *Hope Range* was a coal ship from Broome, only about 10,000 tonnes or so – that's half the size of the *Southern Cross*; she had about a dozen crew and two or three officers. The crew were a mixed bunch from India and Ceylon, though the officers were either English or Australian. She had a diesel engine with massive pistons so big I could park my bike inside. My job was to keep things oiled, wandering around with an oil can and a greasy rag. You could watch the old drive shafts turn slowly at a couple of revolutions a minute, day in day out.

Being the sixth engineer, I even had my own cabin. They turfed out one of the cabin boys and that really put his nose out of joint. About four days into the voyage I got back from a shift and found that someone had rifled through all my gear. I'd put my pistol in the drawer under the bunk, and now it was gone. I reckoned it was the cabin boy talking revenge.

I didn't think there was much chance of getting the pistol back, but that evening I was asked to see the captain on the bridge. He put on the pompous voice that officers use to tick off the crew and informed me that he'd be 'retaining the pistol in his care and hand it to the customs department in Australia.'

I wasn't pleased about that, but there wasn't much I could do about it. The captain gave the pistol to Australian customs, and the Australian customs gave it to New Zealand customs, New Zealand customs gave it to the New Zealand police and they gave me the option of them holding on to it indefinitely, or them destroying it. It was a souvenir as far as I was concerned – I mean, what was the point? Besides, you don't need that sort of thing in New Zealand. I think they destroyed it.

When I finally arrived back in Christchurch on 15 January 1959, my health had deteriorated and I was down to 40 kg. But the trip had been well worth it. I'd met some wonderful people and never got stuck for help. Whenever I broke down there was always a helping hand. Wherever you are, in tiny little mud garages in the remotest places, people will push and pull and bend and heat to help you get things back together. And if you don't speak the lingo, you can always make yourself understood with a few signs and a smile – and perhaps the occasional rupee.

# PASSPORT

The old-fashioned passports read:

'The Administrator of the Government of New Zealand requests and requires in the name of Her Majesty the Queen all those whom it may concern to allow the bearer to pass freely without let or hindrance and to afford the bearer such assistance and protection as may be necessary for a British Subject and New Zealand Citizen.'

# TRICKS OF THE TRADE

*Brian Phillips met his wife Robyn in London in 1964. They were both originally from Wellington, and both on their OE when they met. On his arrival, Brian soon found work as a maintenance carpenter for a London hotel.*

Pete was an Australian carpenter working at one of the posh hotels in London. I met him in a bar, Soho way I think, and we got talking.

I said I was a carpenter, too, and that I was looking for a job. He said, 'You can have mine. I'm off to Paris next week. Can't stand London, weather's bloody awful, the birds are tight and the beer's piss-awful warm.'

We shook on it. I turned up the following morning, was given the briefest of interviews by a world-weary manager and had myself a job. Pete was to stay on a week to show me the ropes – but I suspect the type of tricks he did teach me is not what the hotel had in mind.

My job was to do general repairs and most of the work was mundane – fix this, replace that, sort of general odd jobbery. But the hotel also owned several nightclubs, and it was the carpenter's task to repair the chairs and tables from the club.

'Here,' Pete said, 'you get these chairs in all the time. Buggers always leaning back in them.'

He grinned. 'Keeps you in a job. When you knock 'em apart to re-glue, don't put too much on, see. Just leave the ends dry like this.'

From a pile, he took a chair in various states of disrepair. The rails were hanging loose, and the legs were splayed. A couple of quick taps and both the rail and the legs were in pieces.

'Yup,' he said, squinting down at the inside end of one of the rails. 'Last did this one in June. I put a date on the end so I can see them when they come back in.'

He took down the glue pot and dabbed a plainly insufficient quantity of the sticky stuff on to the tenon, tapped the rails back into place, gave the joint a feeble jerk and put the chair back on the pile for return to the club: 'Doesn't pay to use too much glue, or you'll soon be out of a job.'

Room maintenance was Paddy's job. I don't know whether that was his real name, but he was Irish, so that is what we called him. Paddy was a generous soul and always in the money: every night down at the pub, lunch times in the TAB, always one for a flutter on the horses or the dogs, and never short of a bob or two in between times.

We couldn't work out how he did it. I was a skilled man and on about £10 a week; he wasn't skilled, so he wasn't on trade rates. I suppose he would have been paid the equivalent of about £6 a week. How did he manage the lifestyle?

Then one day, we were swapping tales down in the workshop when the call light went on.

'That'll be for me,' said Paddy and off he went. He was back in 10 minutes, carrying a light bulb and pockets jingling with small change. He put the bulb carefully in his locker and, grinning fit to bust, announced that he was off to the pub.

I couldn't believe it. 'Again? You're always down at the pub, how do you manage it?'

He wasn't going to tell me, but I prodded and pried and eventually he sold the yarn. He had this thing going with the receptionist. Every morning, they'd check the books. Any Americans due and Paddy would collect his light bulb from the locker, wander into the room booked by the American guests and replace the bulb above the bed with the dud.

Then he'd wait for the call. In would walk the Americans, put their bags onto the rack, turn on the light and remark: 'Durn, the light don't work. Mavis, call room service.'

So up goes Paddy to replace the bulb and receive a generous tip for his prompt, efficient and courteous service.

'It only works with Americans, though,' he said, 'It's not worth trying with your lot or the Aussies, and as for the Brits – they're as tight as, eh.'

Half a dozen fiddles like that kept Paddy in the three bees – beer, baccie and the betting shop.

# BUNDLED WITH HAFSTEIN'S MAMA

Jocelyn Macdonald is a third-generation New Zealander, who always knew she would travel to the UK. Her father, a New Zealander by birth, still regarded England as home. Besides, travel was 'what you did post-university and pre-settling down into comfortable respectability'.

Jocelyn left New Zealand in 1963, travelling on the RANGITANE, which was an immigrant ship bound for London. After all the usual things – 'nannying for mad count in Austria, hitchhiking through Portugal and Spain, getting lost in Morocco' – Jocelyn landed a job teaching in Edinburgh.

She and another New Zealand woman, Wendy Peterson, were staying in the Edinburgh Youth Hostel. By spring 1964 they were thoroughly bored and disenchanted with the Scottish life and weather. Two American youths staying in the hostel at the same time as them boasted of the huge sums of money that could be made working on the fishing fleet in Iceland. They'd arrived in the UK with their wallets bulging and their friendly brashness at full volume.

It sounded very exotic compared with damp, cold Edinburgh in January. After a dreadful day with Edinburgh eight-year-olds, Jocelyn and Wendy walked into the Icelandic Consulate to arrange visas, passage from Glasgow to Reykjavik and jobs. Within two weeks, they'd boarded a small boat heading for Iceland to work in a fish-processing plant.

*Hafsteinn, his mama and two brothers.*

It wasn't a long passage and the weather wasn't that bad, but it was a very small boat – much smaller than the Inter-islander. So we were rather relieved to arrive in Reykjavik. We found a bus out to Keflavik, the international airport, about 40 km from Reykjavik, and then on to Sandgerdi on the west coast of the Reykjanes peninsula.

It was grand: the feel, the smell and the look of the place. Barren rocks interspersed with light, lichen greens. Mountains tumbling in huge scree slopes to the valleys. Great sheets of water reflecting the huge dome of the sky. The colours were so different; we had this sense of space and of light. After the grime of Edinburgh and Glasgow it was exhilarating.

It was just as well that we felt enchanted with the place as the road from Keflavik to Sandgerdi was shocking. It was an unmetalled, deeply rutted track. There were large, jagged stones and our decrepit bus shook and rattled noisily up the hills. Sandgerdi was a village of just over 1000 people, sitting at the head of a small inlet. There were neat two-storey houses roofed with tin (how New Zealand) jumbled higgledy-piggledy around the bay; their colours reflected in huge sheets of water. Behind the village, the mountains were still covered with snow. There was little vegetation, no trees, and few fences.

The fish-processing plant was a battered wooden and corrugated iron building precariously perched by the wharf. Fish were off-loaded from the boats and swung up into the 'factory' where the workers would fillet and process cod and capelin.

There were about 30 workers, mostly from the Faroes and Iceland. The 'locals' followed the fishing fleet around the island. The work wasn't that onerous; it was smelly but you soon got used to it. Most of us were under 25, so there were many high jinks – dropping cod eyeballs down people's necks, flicking fish bones around, rides in the wheelbarrow, that sort of thing. We lived in a big hostel across the road from the factory.

Life in the hostel was fun but uncomfortable. Lunch would consist of one of two dishes: boiled mutton and potatoes or boiled fish and potatoes. If we had mutton for lunch, then it was fish for tea. If we had fish for lunch, then it was mutton for tea. By the end of a week, we would have killed for a banana.

We were the first New Zealanders in this part of Iceland, and other English speakers were a rare breed. Neither of us spoke Icelandic or any of the other Nordic languages, and we never really got past the basic greeting stage.

'Góðan dag, one would say.

'Hvað segirðu gott?' the other would reply.

All we could do was smile and nod and hope that our *jas* and *neis* were in approximately the right places. The mutual mis-understanding got us into various scrapes, all of which were resolved with good humour.

At weekends we would all cram into a dilapidated taxi, usually an ageing American Pontiac or Chevy, and drive two to three hours to one of the other villages for a dance or grand fisherman or farmer party. Needless to say that two young New Zealand and one South African women were at the centre of attraction. The Sandgerdi fishing population, and that of the other villages, consisted of a large number of single males, who had nothing much to do other than to drink to excess and lean on the wharf and ogle. A succession of hopeful lads was always queuing up to buy us drinks and ask for dances in broken English and giggling Icelandic.

One such lad was called Hafsteinn. He had lovely curly hair and green eyes. He was a very personable young man who spoke a limited amount of English; not much better than my Icelandic, but certainly a lot better than no conversation at all.

One weekend, he invited me to meet his family. They lived about two or three hours' drive to the east along a bone-shaking track. He had three brothers, all living with his parents in a tiny farmhouse. The family ran a horticulture business growing tomatoes in thermally heated glass houses and they also herded a few sheep on local pasture.

'Mama' didn't speak English at all, so the conversation was mediated through Hafsteinn. Goodness only knows what was lost in translation. First Mama would beam and smile: 'Það gleður mig að kynnast þér.'

And Hafsteinn would say, 'Mama is very pleased to meet you.'

Then Mama would say, 'Má bjóða þér fleiri kartöflur?'

And her son would translate, 'Would you like some more potatoes?'

And I'd reply, 'No thank you, I have had quite enough.' I was a very well brought-up Kiwi.

Then Mama would rattle off, 'Hvað áttu marga bræður og systur á Nýja Sjálandi?'

And Hafsteinn would translate, 'Do you have a family in New Zealand?'

And I'd reply, 'Two brothers and a sister. 'Tvo bræður og eina systur.'

And so it went on. But from the odd looks I got by early evening, I suspected Hafstein's English limited the accuracy of the translation.

We'd finished tea and I was beginning to yawn. Mama went to a cupboard and took out a bottle of the local spirit. This is an extremely powerful drink, rather like schnapps, and a great many of the young Islandic men drink rather too much of it.

Mama charged our glasses, beamed at me and announced, 'ðú ert mjög falleg,' patting my arm and beaming with a delighted smile. Back came the translation, 'Mama says you are very beautiful.'

Mama went on, 'Mikið er ég fegin að Hafsteinn hefur loksins fundið sér góða konu. Ég hlakka svo til að hitta mömmu þína elskan. Við skulum hafa glæsilegt kirkjubrúðkaup og þú getur unnið í gróðurhúsinu. Hvað um það, ég er þreytt. Þið Hafsteinn getið verið í bakherberginu. Sofið vel.'*

Hafsteinn was grinning from ear to ear by this stage and looking very pleased with himself. But when I heard the translation I shot bolt upright: 'Mama is very pleased to have you as a daughter. Mama says because we are now engaged you can sleep with me.'**

I didn't need any translation to express my dismay, worry and embarrassment. I just about choked on my schnapps. So there was more rapid Icelandic and, fortunately, a lot of laughter.

'Mama says that if you don't want to sleep with me, you can sleep with her.'

---

* The exact transalation is: 'Well I am so pleased Hafsteinn has found a nice lady at long last. I am so looking forward to meeting your mother, dear. We will have a grand church wedding and you can work in the tomato house. Anyway I'm tired. You and Hafsteinn can have the back room. Sleep well.'

** In Icelandic society, several other northern European countries and even in puritan New England, it was considered acceptable, indeed even encouraged, for engaged couples to sleep together. It proved fertility and the evidence for the practice can be found in timing of births and marriages in parish registers all over England. In pre Victorian England and in the early days of the American colonies, the practice was called bundling.

I didn't really have much of a choice. This was a very small house. So I followed Mama down the corridor to a room with a huge double bed and the first duvet I'd ever seen. Mama pulled open the covers and delved under a pillow. Out came this huge, voluminous and fortunately very modest tent of a nightie. I put it on and hopped into bed with Mama. Then, talking all the while, she delved under the pillow again, this time to produce a bag of lollies. She hardly had time to change into her nightclothes herself, when Hafsteinn arrived and hopped into the other end of the bed.

So there were the three of us. Hafsteinn, Hafstein's mama and I, all sitting in bed celebrating mutual misunderstanding with a bag of lollies. All the while Mama was rattling way in Icelandic, patting my arm and beaming with her hope for a future daughter-in-law. Forlorn hope.

We travelled back to Sangerdi the following day. There wasn't a great deal of any sort of conversation on the way back. I gathered from one of the other workers that Hafsteinn had been 'engaged' several times before and even had a child (or several) in one of the villages.

Wendy and I stayed at Sangerdi until May. It was a very special time; so much fun, and very sociable despite the language barrier: the weekend dance parties, walks on the beach, living in the hostel. I regret that I didn't get up north, but the whole trip had a magic feel to it.

# PHEASANTS AND POTATOES

John Stemmer's forebears had travel in their blood. First they emigrated from Austria to England around 1750, then members of the family settled in New Zealand in 1870.

John's first job, after he'd left school, was with Sladen's, a diamond merchant and watch importer in Cathedral Square, Christchurch. The son of the founder of the firm had by then retired, but spent all his money on travelling. He had been around the world nine times by ship. There was a large map of the world on the wall in the smoko room and the owners spent all their time talking about travel.

It was infectious so, before long, John and his mate Roger Bamford booked a passage on the FAIRSEA on July 1st, 1962. It was a strange scene: a huge crowd on the Auckland waterfront bidding farewell to an Italian ship. There were streamers and a band playing 'Waltzing Matilda', and lots of tears and emotions running high. Six weeks later, John and Roger arrived in Southampton.

I earned the fare to England in two long weekends – decoking the funnel of a Blue Star freighter in Lyttelton. We made £85, which was extraordinary money for those days. Once on board the *Fairsea*, all we had do was buy booze and colour films. There were about 1200 passengers and many were our age, with an equal split between the genders. It was one six-week party. Great fun.

As soon as we arrived in London, we headed for the Overseas Visitors Club. They had a branch in Earls Court Road, where you could get room and board and find a job. There was a bar, and many of us colonials – Australians, New Zealanders, Canadians, South Africans and Rhodesians – to make everyone feel at home.

*Roger, John and their friend Bob (front) with Mike and Phil Buck (back) at Tresco.*

Needless to say, it was raining when we arrived (August Bank Holiday) and we were soon complaining about the weather. One of the guys at the Club said there were jobs on a farming estate in the Scilly Islands, where it was rather more tropical. That sounded like a good deal, so once we'd made the arrangements, we caught a train and headed down to the West Country.

The Isles of Scilly were a little group of 30 or so islands 44 km from Land's End. There were five inhabited islands, the two main ones being St Mary's and Tresco. The main port was St Mary's and we had to go by whaling boat to get to Tresco. The tide was dead low and as we threaded our way through channels, little islands and rocks, we wondered what on earth we were coming to.

Tresco port was a small tidal bay with one stone jetty. It had a dozen or so houses around the beach and a pub and a hotel on the other side of the island. As we arrived at the beach, a bearded, sturdy-looking fellow in boots and old clothes appeared. When we got off the boat, he held out his hand and said, 'I'm Bob Adams from Patea. Put it there, mate.' I thought, 'Here we are, just about as remote from anywhere as you can get, and here is a guy from

Patea.' He showed us to our lodging, then took us off to meet the other workers in the pub.

There were the two Buck brothers from Melbourne. They were hard case, one tall and rangy the other short and broad, both good-looking Aussie guys. There were several South African girls, another Kiwi, two Aussie girls, and an English and an Irish girl; about a dozen or so youngsters all working in the hotel or on the Tresco Abbey Estate.

The Abbey Estate covered the island and was owned by Lieutenant Commander TM Dorian-Smith RN (retired). He was a cousin of the Queen and rode around on a push-bike, wearing his captain's hat, a double-breasted jacket with silver buttons, a carnation in his button hole, black trousers and sea boots. Extraordinary – and so different from home.

The commander lived in Tresco Abbey; we were told he was married to a Russian princess. He had two daughters – the Buck boys from Melbourne had their eyes on them, for sure, but the daughters were steering clear. They came from a different social scene, but there was much talk and laughter in the pub.

The estate ran a few animals, grew acres of early daffodils for the mainland and export markets, and owned the pub, hotel, all the houses and shops, a museum of shipwrecks and a botanical garden. One of the commander's ancestors had brought back a collection of plants from the South Seas, including cabbage trees and tree ferns. But it didn't seem to be an intensive operation. In those days, tourism was only just beginning and it was fairly quiet for the time we were there.

There were no cars on the island; the only motorised transport consisted of noisy little three-wheel mopeds, which towed a trailer; a sort of primitive quad bike and a couple of tractors and trailers. All the produce would be taken down to the wharf on these little mopeds, loaded on to double-ended lighters and barged to St Mary's before going on to the mainland. Everything – the food for the island, booze for the pub, concrete – was shifted in and out by those lighters.

Roger and I were billeted with an old lady who treated us like long-lost grandsons. She lived in a two-storey stone house at Old Grimsby, on the far side of the island. The meals were hearty. We could come back from work to see her wading in the bay, skirts hitched up round her waist, wielding a shrimping net to catch supper. Board was £3 a week and the estate gave her an extra 10s. for each billet

We were paid between £9 and £11 a week, including overtime. We did a bit of everything, from digging daffodil bulbs or collecting tickets for the museum, to unloading the lighters. The estate supervisor was an ex-army sergeant-major. When the lighters came in, you could just about hear his bellow from one end of the island to the other: 'We'll have the strong-armed colonial boys down on the wharf. Wind those winches, boys – let's put some muscle on you.' But it was all good-natured.

Early on in our stay, one beautiful summer's evening, Roger and I were set to work lifting spuds. There were pheasants everywhere – we'd never seen so many in one place.

One other permanent staff member was the gamekeeper. He was an officious man, big moustache, always dressed up in his plus-fours and tweed hat; always in a bad temper. You'd see him in the distance carrying a basket of grain. He'd trained all the pheasants to come to a call – he'd sit down behind a wall and play a little flute to whistle in the birds and within a few minutes they'd all come rocketing out of the hedgerows to get their evening feed. They were more like pets than wild birds.

This was odd to us, but what was even weirder was that at the end of the summer the commander would get all these old buffers from the mainland – colonels and admirals and knights and everything – and they'd have a shoot. These pheasants were so fat, someone would have to throw the poor things in the air from behind a wall before they could be targeted. No wonder the gamekeeper was bad tempered – he spent all his time raising the birds, feeding them up and playing to them on his flute, and some other buggers come along and shot them. Bizarre.

Well, we didn't know any of that at the time. We were just two lads from Christchurch who didn't know you raised pheasants. We didn't know anything about shoots and shooting and country 'sports'. And we certainly didn't know that it was okay for a colonel or knight to shoot a tame pheasant, but not for two lads from Christchurch to knock one off for supper.

All we knew was that we were in a field and there were pheasants everywhere and we'd never seen anything like it. We looked at each other and Roger said, 'Let's see if we can pot one of these for tea.' We grabbed as many spuds as our hands would hold, and let fly. It was a huge joke. There were spuds and pheasants going in all directions.

We were cracking up with laughter, when the gamekeeper put his head over the wall, moustache wiggling and fit to burst a blood vessel with rage. 'What the devil do you think you are doing?' he bellowed.

Roger was never one to turn aside from an argument and he took a really aggressive stance: feet apart and hands on hips. 'What the hell do you mean?' he bellowed back.

'How dare you disturb my game!'

And Roger was back into it yelling, 'Where we come from we bowl them over and put them in a pot.'

And the gamekeeper is shouting back fit to bust, 'Where do you come from then?'

'New Zealand,' was the reply at 100 decibels plus.

And this fellah says, 'Well get right back there now,' and he turns on his heel and stomps back up the lane.

'Jeez,' we thought, 'we're in trouble now. Might be on our way tomorrow.'

So we finished up lifting spuds and headed back to the pub, feeling rather subdued. By the time we got down to the port, the news had gone before us. The Buck brothers and the girls were leaning on the bar as we walked, all turning towards us with huge grins on their faces.

'Can't have a couple of Kiwis on the island for more than two minutes and they're in trouble!' They wound us up something terrible. Boy, we were going to get our wages docked. They'd probably shove us in St Mary's jail. Wasn't a medieval crime of cruelty to pheasants still on the statute books? Probably need the thumbscrews. Wouldn't like to be in your shoes. On and on they went.

But it all blew over, though we tried to avoid the gamekeeper for the rest of our stay, and we were never asked to lift potatoes again.

# GOLD SOVEREIGNS

*Laurie Polglase was born and bred in Hamilton but wanted to go to England before he even knew where it was: 'I thought it was near Auckland. My grandfather came from Preston in Lancashire and I didn't know where that was, either. After leaving school I did a joinery apprenticeship and later swapped to cabinet making, which came in useful in the UK.'*

I got a berth on the MV *Ruahine* to England in the mid-1960s. She was an old ship in her 25th year of service and we broke down in the Pacific and then again in the Atlantic. We were threatened by Cuban gunboats in the straits of Florida – that was an interesting story in itself.

We made it to London and I eventually went to stay with my great-uncle Tom in Preston. It wasn't long before my money dried up, so I did what thousands of New Zealanders have done before and since . . . I got a job. A trip overseas isn't really all that meaningful if you don't work and mix with the people in their own environment.

I went to the Labour Exchange and said I wanted a cabinet-making job. The clerk behind the counter looked at me as if I was mad and pulled out a thick file of jobs. Apparently the English didn't want to work, they would rather be on the benefit. So I chose the job that was closest to where I lived and had the best pay.

I fronted up to the address in Market Street the next morning at 8 am. R Walker & Son was a jobbing builder – a dismal sort of place, real north-of-England in the gloom and drizzle.

There was a two-storey façade, itself at least 200 years old, and a dimly lit front office. There didn't seem to be anybody around so

The MV RUAHINE.

I went in, banged on the door and called, 'Anyone there?', and waited.

A tall, well-dressed man wafted out of the gloom and asked if I was a New Zealander.

'Yes, sir,' I said.

'Kiwi, you've got the job.' He asked no questions, didn't want to know what I could do, or wanted do, just said, 'You've got the job.'

Later, when we sat down to discuss it, it turned out that Walker senior had been with New Zealanders in the war, and he'd been so well looked after that he vowed that if a Kiwi ever crossed his doorstep, he could have a job.

Walker senior was a cranky gentleman, but he was always pleasant to me. He took great interest in New Zealand and I found him easy to get on with.

Walker junior was more relaxed, but he ran the business with his chequebook zipped so tight you'd think the light bulbs were for decoration. I expect the secretary used a candle for light and warmth. Father and son drove late-model Jaguars you'd hardly dare look at. Mere workers were forbidden almost to look and I was probably the only employee ever to ride in one.

Back then, England was still fairly structured. The class system went all the way down: a builder did the concrete work, a joiner did the structural building and a cabinetmaker stayed in the workshop and made the windows, doors, furniture and so forth. I used to get told off for not calling the boss 'sir'. I explained that 'sir' was no longer used in the colonies and that I wasn't about to start it up again.

In the three months that I worked for the Walkers, I managed to get out on several outside jobs. I had an apprentice, Mike, assigned to me. He was a likeable lad and, like all apprentices, had plenty of time for socialising, though not much for his studies. One of our first jobs was to cut an archway in the wall of an old manor house.

The owner was joining two rooms with an archway. He was a nice enough guy – about 50 or so and more than willing to yarn – but I was more interested in the history of the house.

It had been built in about 1100 AD and was showing its age. The floorboards creaked, doors chattered on dry hinges, floors sagged and walls leaned. The interior walls were about 30 cm thick and made of hand-hewn timber mortised and tenoned together. This framing was lined both sides with strips of wood (battens) and a very thick layer of plaster on top: an ancient system called 'lath and plaster'.

After 900 years of drying out, the plaster was very flaky and dusty. We had to close the doors and windows and block the gaps with paper to prevent the dust from getting into the rest of the house. Since it was so hot, we stripped down to our shorts and wrapped our shirts around our faces to stop breathing the grey white dust, but we still ended up looking like ghosts.

As the plaster was removed, some interesting things came to light: the skeleton of a rat that could have carried the plague, the remains of a bird trapped centuries ago, a long-abandoned wasps' nest, lots of pennies, halfpennies and farthings. Right down on the bottom plate was a pile of black metal disks just a little bigger than our 10-cent piece, only a bit thicker and much heavier. We swept them up with the rest of the rubbish and put them in the skip.

At lunchtime, we washed up and went outside into the sun.

Mike had given the copper coins to the owner, but kept one of the black disks. He was idly rubbing it on his trousers when the old washer started to gleam. We looked carefully. Mike rubbed a bit more and looked again.

It was a gold sovereign, gleaming and glittering in the sun.

We looked at each other, then at the coin, and then we were up, tea and sandwiches flying in all directions in our haste to get back into the skip and find the other disks. We emptied the entire skip and found about 40 more of them.

This created a bit of a dilemma for me. As the one in charge, I had to be honest and report such a find. We sat down and discussed the pros and cons of keeping a coin each and handing in the rest. I knew I couldn't take one out of the country, but . . . It was tempting, but you just have to be honest. So we called the owner over to show him what we'd found.

He was 'a study' in changed attitude. Friendship to lust for gold – quite remarkable. Still friendly but not so friendly when he thought we were going to claim his gold. We had already given him the copper coins – no way was he going to share these with anyone. (Gold coins belong to the nation. They weren't his to take any more than they were mine to pinch.)

I was duty bound to report the find to the boss, which I did, and left it in his capable hands. I did say that if there was a reward I'd appreciate some of it for being honest. Mike wrote to me a few years later and said there was a compensation sum paid for the coins, but he got none of it and neither did I.

Should I have pinched one gold sovereign?

# FLY SPRAY AND HAKAS

Ray Amer left school at 15 to work on Canterbury farms. He came from a rugby league family and his brother played for the Kiwis on a tour of Britain and France in 1962. Besides admiring prominent sportspersons, Ray remembers envying schoolteachers and nurses who seemed to be able to pack their skills and a small suitcase to travel and adventure.

In early 1960, Ray met an Australian merchant seaman rousting his way around the world. He persuaded Ray to work a passage to the UK via Sydney and Perth.

After a stint of painting houses in Sydney, Ray, an Australian called Mervyn Apps and an English nurse, Marion Hazard, teamed up to cross the Nullabor Plain. They bought a 1926 Chevy truck, stocked up with water, sardines, two sacks of rice and a tonne of ignorance, and set off west for Perth. On the way the axle broke, the wheel fell off and after three months, the engine and the travellers just about blew themselves apart.

It took six months before Mervyn and Ray could speak to each other again, and Marion simply disappeared. They haven't heard of her since. But Mervyn and Ray eventually made it to the UK on an old troop ship, the STRATHNAVAR. In the UK, Ray met his wife-to-be Jill and, in 1962, they decided to return to New Zealand.

But that first trip, and the ego-boosting publicity about the oldest vehicle ever to cross the Nullabor, wetted Ray's appetite for slow travel in old bangers. Consequently, Jill and Ray decided to drive to India. Ray liked old cars and persuaded Jill, who hadn't a clue what she was letting herself in for, to do the trip in a classic car.

The previous year, an English pair had driven a 1934 Riley from

*London to Delhi. Ray wasn't about to let the English beat him in the old car stakes. He managed to find a 1933 Morris 10 in mint condition – and for only £25. With some modification, it would do.*

*The couple left Britain in 1963, following the Marco Polo trail. By the time they arrived in Delhi, Jill had a better idea of what she was letting herself in for, and the Morris 10 had lost its pristine sheen.*

*While they were travelling through Turkey, they camped one night on a lonely plateau. Ray tells the story of the fly spray, the haka and the gypsy queen.*

I suppose we were both a bit hung over. We'd had a marvellous farewell from our Turkish host, Nuri, the previous night. Fed, fêted and fezed, the hospitality had been just amazing, with about a dozen courses of rich food: sweetmeats, aubergines swimming in oil, spiced meat dishes, and endless cups of coffee in little copper cups. So we thought we'd head south across the Anatolian plain towards the Mediterranean coast, to swim and recover before the next stage of the journey through Jordan and on into Iraq.

We didn't want to go far that night – the unsealed road (no more than a track) was dusty and dirty, and we were hot and bothered and had been shaken around in the Morris. The springs weren't really designed for this type of trip, so by four o'clock we were ready to stop for the night.

This part of Turkey was very barren. It was a plateau of limestone at about 1500 m altitude between the coast and mountains 200 km to the east. The soils were thin, so there was little arable agriculture. There were a few villages of beehive-shaped mud huts and most of the people herded sheep and goats for a living. What water there was flowed through deep limestone gorges. The colours and shapes were such a contrast to the flat, lush plains of Canterbury, or Jill's green Yorkshire dales.

We had passed through a few villages and it seemed safe enough to camp for the night, so we pulled the Morris over to the side of the road. There was no one in sight – not a goat, not a herder, and all was quiet. The sun was beginning to lose some of its heat, so Jill took out the gas stove and the cooking gear while I set up the tent.

We hadn't been there more than 10 minutes, when we heard the sound of horses and rapid talk. A group of gypsies – four men, a woman and a couple of small children – came galloping over from a small rise about a kilometre away. I suppose they must have been watching us from there.

The men were extremely shabby: drab black trousers and jackets, dirty, yellow-oil shirts and leather boots. They had unkempt hair, full moustaches and eyes of dark, dark brown set in bloodshot whites. The horses were the best-kept part of the group – Arab-type animals with saddles decorated in beads and braid in brilliant colour.

The woman was, I'd say, in her mid-thirties. She had a full, fit figure, just like I'd imagined a gypsy queen would, with black flowing hair and a dark complexion. She wore a full skirt and a dramatic scarf that must have been over a square metre in size around her shoulders.

At first the gypsies were all smiles, laughter and flashing teeth, riding around the tent and car, pointing and gibbering away in Romany. Needless to say, we couldn't understand a word they said, and vice versa, I presume. We laughed and smiled in return, but kept a close eye on them and closed all but one of the doors in the Morris.

After a few minutes and some conversation in Romany, the woman dismounted and began to dance. She moved as you would expect, swaying her hips sinuously from side to side, using the scarf as a prop, sweeping it in front of her face and body, clicking small tambourines on her fingers; beguiling, to the wail and the rhythm of a song about we knew not what. The men swaggered on their horses, chanting and snapping their fingers in time.

It seemed wonderful: a completely unexpected entertainment at the end of a tiring day. It was exotic; it was fascinating. But about 10 minutes after the dancing began, the floor show ended abruptly. There was more rapid-fire speech in Romany, now directed at us.

The woman began to advance, holding out her hands in a

*Ray and Jill with the Morris 10 entering Pakistan.*

begging gesture. There was no mistaking the message. We were expected to pay.

But we had no money. We had only £100 for the entire trip and we'd blown most of our dinars in Ankara. I wasn't keen to dip into the reserves for an unasked-for dance performance.

Jill delved into the Morris and came out with a box of Turkish delight our hosts in Ankara had given us for the journey. She walked towards the woman, proffering the sweets, thinking that it might calm things down.

Far from it. The woman struck the box from Jill's hand, scattering Nuri's gift across the dirt.

Now the tone of the voices began to change; it was harder, more demanding. The woman was getting closer and closer, arguing and stabbing the fingers of one hand into the palm of the other while the men were muttering, setting up a background murmur to intimidate and threaten.

Jill looked shocked and frightened and backed away. I began to wonder if the Morris could outpace an Arab horse and looked around for help. There was none. If these four chose to attack us, we were in trouble and there was not a great deal we could do about it.

When I turned round again, Jill was leaning inside the car, no longer looking frightened, but furious. 'How dare they refuse my sweets?' her expression was telling me. 'How dare they throw them on the ground!'

The gypsy woman was now approaching Jill's side of the car. I'd stayed by the driver's side, within reach of my bayonet. Before we left, we'd had discussions on self-defence. A gun was obviously out of the question, but I bought an old World War II bayonet from an army surplus store in Bradford. It was the only decent weapon I could think of. I kept it in the driver's side pocket and if push came to shove, I reckoned, I'd give an account of myself.

Jill came out backwards, turned and marched towards the woman, bristling with anger, and about to give as good as she had been getting. 'If you don't go away, I'll give you something to drive you off,' she snapped. She pointed something at the gypsy woman. There was more angry Romany, more angry English. Jill had grabbed the only thing she could find at the time – our can of fly spray. Phssst. Jill pressed the trigger and a stream of insect repellent wafted in the gypsy queen's direction.

There was a momentary pause in the Romany tirade. Whether from shock, surprise, or just sheer bamboozlement, the troupe seemed to go into a temporary suspended animation. It was a weird scene: four moustachioed gypsy horsemen on fine Arab mounts, two dirty children and a gypsy queen holding a large scarf in one hand and a tambourine in the other, with a look of shocked surprise as she wondered what the funny smell was.

Unfortunately, Bug Off might work on mosquitoes but it is no substitute for pepper spray. So, within a few seconds, the diatribe began again. Now one of the horsemen was beginning to get off his horse. The other three were looking uneasy, the children worried. On and on the woman went, throwing her hand in the air, stabbing her palm, making demanding, threatening gestures, spitting her words at Jill.

This had gone far enough. I reached inside the door pocket of the Morris and grabbed the bayonet. I walked around the car, stamped the ground and launched into the haka of Te Rauparaha.

*Ka mate, ka mate! Ka ora, ka ora!*

*Tenei te tangata uhuruhuru*

I was bellowing the words, slapping my thighs with one hand, stamping the ground with my feet; rolling my eyes, poking out my tongue and trying to avoid sticking myself with the bayonet, which I waved at the men on horseback. Giving it all it was worth: 10 years of training on the stony fields of Canterbury rugby coming to the fore.

I roared, I thundered, I threatened:

*Nana nei i tiki mai*

*I whakawhiti te ra*

*Upane, Upane*

*Upane, ka upane*

*Whiti te ra!*

Well, the queen did back off. Boy did she ever. She was on her horse with one fluid motion. And so were her moustachioed friends, while the horses carrying their alarmed mounts shot backwards. I must have been quite a sight: a mad Kiwi in khaki shorts and tatty T-shirt advancing on a group of five mounted gypsies waving a bayonet and yelling fit to burst. They were off in a cloud of dust, and when the hoofbeats faded away, we leant against the Morris shaking with relief, not knowing whether to laugh or cry.

We didn't stop around either. In fact, we've never packed so fast. No way were we camping there that night – instead we decided to drive to the coast and sleep in the car rather than hang around waiting for the queen and her courtiers to return.

# LAUNCHING THE *WAIKATO*

There were Gwen, Rosemary, Roslyn, Raewyn, Rosemary, Relda and Kerry, all of whom came from either the Waikato or Taranaki. Early in 1964, the girls bought a Bedford van, called it GRRRRRK, painted 'New Zealand' across the front and loaded it up with seven females, seven suitcases, seven sleeping bags, two large tents, two primus stoves, and two large Pipkin beer cans to be used as cooking pots. They travelled through Scandinavia into the Arctic Circle, Lapland, south to Moscow, Poland, Germany, behind the Iron Curtain to Hungary, Bulgaria, Romania, on to Turkey and back to Britain through Greece, Yugoslavia, Italy and Spain.

Rosemary Bennett and friends on their 'big OE'.

While we lived in London, we picked up our mail from New Zealand House. On one visit early in 1965, we discovered that Waikato people could get invitations to the launching of the HMNZS *Waikato*. That might be interesting, we thought.

We applied for tickets and were duly issued with numbered blue invitations to the 'Launching of the HMNZS *Waikato* by Her Royal Highness Princess Alexandra on Thursday, 18 February 1965' at the Abercorn Shipyard in Belfast – appropriately at the Hamilton Dock No 1.

A few weeks before the launch, we drove to Liverpool and caught the ferry to Belfast. We hired a van and made a grand circle of Ireland though Dublin, Cork, Killarney, then up the west coast though Londonderry and back to Belfast.

The 'troubles' had not yet started. There was no sign of violence – no bombed-out buildings, no army checkpoints and we were free to travel back and forth across the border as we pleased. We thought it was beautiful, green and lush; not unlike parts of New Zealand, but with stone walls, quaint buildings, peat fires, donkey carts, and gypsies with horse-drawn caravans to remind us that this was Ireland.

In contrast, Belfast was just another drab, industrial town much like any other in Britain's industrial north. The Abercorn Shipyard was part of Harland and Wolff Ltd. The company had built famous passenger ships like the *Titanic* and the *Canberra*, and many warships for the Royal Navy.

Our tickets instructed us to arrive at the 'Reserves Stand' of the shipyard by 11.15 am. On the way to the shipyard, we had a slight altercation with another vehicle; although there was no serious damage, we had to stop and swap names and addresses. By the time we got to the docks we were running late. We arrived at the gate in a mild panic, trying to discover where we had to go.

There were crowds of people, all pressed behind barriers, with shipyard workers and the public mingling with naval ratings and officers in uniform.

We showed our blue invitations to a traffic policeman and were guided to the reserved stand. We climbed up red-carpeted steps to our places. There we stood, shoulder to shoulder with the naval officers bedecked in gold and braid, dignitaries in dark suits, and wives in fur coats and hats. There was Princess Alexandra, gracious and elegant. There were the Kiwis, dressed warmly in our Sunday best – duffle coats, woolly hats and brightly coloured jackets covered in 'I've been there' badges.

It was all very emotional. There was a short speech, then Princess Alexandra formally spoke: 'I name this ship the HMNZS *Waikato*. May God bless her and all who sail in her.'

A bottle of Te Kauwhata wine swung against the bow and slowly, very slowly, the grey mass began to move. The band played; the workers (on board the *Waikato*'s decks) raised their hats: 'Three cheers for the *Waikato*. Hip hip hooray!' and we all cheered.

Launch of **5**

# H.M.N.Z.S. WAIKATO

by

# HER ROYAL HIGHNESS PRINCESS ALEXANDRA

on Thursday, 18th February, 1965.

## ADMIT ONE

### TO RESERVED STAND

Guests should arrive at the Reserved Stand in Abercorn Shipyard before 11. 15 a.m.

*THIS CARD MUST BE SHOWN ON REQUEST*

The ticket to the launch.

Moist-eyed, we were remembering home, proud to be New Zealanders. Although our generation grew up hearing the UK referred to as 'home', we were Kiwis. We were interviewed after the launching and it felt right to finish it with a rendition of the battle song of the Maori Battalion – the interview was later played on National Radio.

## EPILOGUE

Thirty-three years later, when the HMNZS *Waikato** reached the end of her career, five out of the original seven GRRRRRK attended three decommissioning parade and civic functions in Hamilton and Auckland. On these occasions, the duffle coats, woolly hats and badge-encrusted jackets were nowhere to be seen.

Thirty-three years ago, Relda acquired the neck of the bottle used by Princess Alexandra to launch the ship. She kept the glass, complete with attached ribbons, in her glory box. We mounted the fragments on a piece of wood and returned them to the Naval Museum at Devonport.

---

* The *Waikato* was finally sunk as a diving attraction in 29 metres of water in Tutukaka in the Bay of Islands in November 2000. Strangely enough, at that time five of the group were having a reunion in New Plymouth and so observed a minute's silence for our old friend, the HMNZS *Waikato*.

# HE CARRIES A TYPEWRITER

The Patris was a Greek ship. It was old, and occasionally broke down. There were not many organised amusements on board, but John Robertson did learn how to sing the Greek national anthem, in Greek, to the tune of 'Never On a Sunday'.

John landed at Piraeus in early 1963 then travelled on to Milan, Calais and London by train.

In the early 1960s, the first stop for many New Zealanders and Australians was the Overseas Visitors Club in Earls Court Road. The club could arrange accommodation and find jobs, and there was a bar and a dance floor in the basement. After various jobs in England, John took off on his European trip.

I came up with the idea to take the Orient Express through Belgrade down into Istanbul. I was going to take three months over the whole journey and I could stop off anywhere I liked.

After one stopover, I got back on the train at Udine in Italy, travelled up to Villach, then down to Ljubljana, Zagreb and onto Belgrade. The train was electric as far as Austria, then changed to steam for the journey through Eastern Europe.

The compartments had room for about eight people – four to a side, crammed together on hard wooden seats. The corridor along one side connected the compartments and it was jam-packed as well. It was hardly the flash world of Agatha Christie and the romantic novelists, unless you were in the first class carriage.

And it wasn't an express, either. I think it might have reached 50 kilometres per hour on the straight, but for most of the journey the train rattled, swayed and shook its way round mountains and valleys.

Popovic with the typewriter case.

This left plenty of time to make friends with the other passengers. I found a minute space in one compartment full of young men about my age. The other travellers turned out to be guest workers from Germany heading back to Belgrade in Yugoslavia. They all squeezed up to make space for me and we started talking.

The guy sitting opposite me said he was a teacher. His name was Popovic Svetozav and he was very Slavic looking, slightly balding and dressed in those shabby Eastern European grey trousers and cheap patent leather shoes. But he was charming and educated and, in fluent English, told me he had been teaching in Munich.

We chatted about New Zealand and Yugoslavia and this and that. He then started telling me about how common things in Germany were in short supply in Yugoslavia. One of the good things about being a guest worker, he said, was that you got to take things back to your family – except that customs would usually steal any imported goods for their own private use.

They all looked very gloomy. 'What sort of things?' I asked.

And they laughed and said, 'Everything, everything!'

I found myself packing a stack of toilet paper, odd articles of clothing and one or two other bits and pieces in my backpack. It seemed innocuous – I couldn't see any harm in taking toilet paper across the border.

There was a portable typewriter up in the luggage rack. Popovic took it down, looked very sad and said that customs might have a real problem with it. His companions laughed.

He looked grim and muttered, 'It's okay for a Westerner to use a typewriter but it's not allowed for us,' and then more cheerfully: 'Would you take it through?'

By this time I was getting into the swing of things, so I said, 'Oh yes', and put it with the rest of my luggage. I wouldn't dream of doing that sort of thing these days, but they were nice enough and so pleased and friendly, how could carrying a typewriter be a problem?*

At 2 am the train pulled into a siding at the border crossing and the Yugoslav customs started to work their way down the corridor. They were big, grim-looking men in grey uniforms and very thorough and threatening. Nobody was allowed off the train. Every person had to pull out their identity cards, while they stared at you with blank eyes, and then they looked at the card and then at the bags, and they wanted to know where you were going and where you were coming from and what you were planning to do.

All my companions had gone very quiet, looking in their laps and fiddling with their hands. When they came to our compartment, the officials opened my bags and gave a cursory look inside. Then he

---

\* It is sometimes difficult to believe that at the height of the Cold War, typewriters and even typewriter ribbons were banned imports into Eastern Europe. They could be used to spread subversive information – whole books were reproduced on manual typewriters in Samizdat versions.

motioned at the typewriter case: 'Whose is this?'

'That's mine,' I grinned and mimed a typing action.

'Huh,' he said and held out his hand: 'Passport.' I handed over my passport and we watched with bated breath while he wrote over the stamp. Then he smiled a funny sort of smug smile and handed back the passport.

I looked at the stamp. He had written 'Nosi pisa on masinu' on the side of the page, and the date, 26/7/69.

As soon as he'd moved to the next compartment, I passed the passport to Popovic and asked, 'What's this mean?'

Popovic looked glum and said, 'He's written, "He carries a typewriter".' This meant that when I left the country I had to be carrying a typewriter or I might run into a few problems.

We tossed the predicament around for a while, with everyone looking rather down. Then Popovic said he would go down to the local market and buy a typewriter case. He didn't have any money, but his brother was a young Communist Youth leader and he could arrange things.

I wasn't terribly keen on this idea. It was the height of the Cold War and I was beginning to imagine being taken into a communist jail, never to be seen again. I said, 'Look, I need some bona fides. I could very well pass you the typewriter and never see you again. How do I know you'll turn up?'

So after some discussion, he passed me his identity card. ID cards were very precious; officially he had to carry his card at all times, so passing it over was quite a gesture of trust. We agreed to meet the following evening outside the Hotel Moscow at 4 pm.

I spent most of the day wandering around Belgrade. It is described by some travel writers as the Paris of Eastern Europe, but I found it drab and run down and I was becoming more and more worried. Supposing Popovic didn't turn up? What if he'd been arrested? Or if I was arrested – no one would know where I was. How would I get out? My parents would never know!

At 4 pm I was trying to look inconspicuous opposite the Hotel Moscow, scanning pedestrians and traffic and wondering whether I would spot the secret police before they arrested me. I saw

Popovic across the road and much to my relief he was carrying the promised case. I walked across, feeling very nervous and looking over my shoulder for the police.

He was as pleased as punch to see me. 'Nothing to it,' he said. 'Shouldn't have worried.' He was jaunty and cheerful, and as relieved to get his identity card back as I was to see the case. 'Let's go out for meal. I take you to eat good Yugoslavia food.'

Maybe I was being paranoid, but despite a very nice meal at a Yugoslav restaurant, I could not relax – as I was lugging a beastly typewriter case around Belgrade, half-expecting to run into the grim-looking border guard at any moment.

To give myself some assurance, before I boarded the train, I walked up and down the platform, looking for someone from the West. I found a dark-haired young man with the Stars and Stripes on his backpack. 'You an American?' I asked.

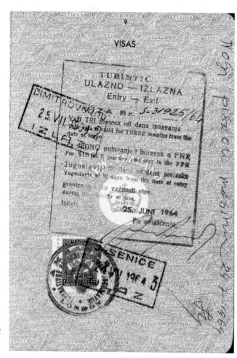

John's passport with the guard's note down the right hand side.

'Sure am.'

I have never been so pleased to hear a New York twang.

As we travelled south, I told him the story and we agreed that if I was arrested he was to tell the British Embassy about it at the next capital town. Before we got to the border, I put all my food in the case. The treatment was the same going out as it was going in: the train was shunted into a siding and grim-faced customs officials worked their way from compartment to compartment. They looked at me, looked at the notation in my passport, looked at the typewriter case, then stamped my passport. I let out a quiet sigh of relief.

Perhaps the paranoia wasn't necessary, but I felt very much at risk in Eastern Europe. Not a good feeling. I mean, what sort of place is it that gets upset over a typewriter?

# LONS-LE-SAUNIER

*Meg Collins was born and raised in Wellington. She'd always had a yen for travel, and left home as soon as she had saved the fare, in 1965. She travelled to London on the* RANGITOTO: *'It was a giant party for five weeks – one of the passengers was a wonderful pianist.' She returned to New Zealand on the* ANGELINA LAURO *in 1967.*

Early in 1966, I applied for an au pair job in France, advertised in one of the English papers. There was no immediate reply, so I joined a three-week trip to Morocco with a group of about six other travellers. It was a great trip and even though we broke down frequently, the group didn't. The weather was hot and dry, we were dirty and dusty most of the time, but we visited many odd places in our old, clapped-out Commer van, and it was an experience to remember.

I had arranged for my mail to be forwarded to Tangier. On the way back from Morocco, I collected the mail and, in with the letters from the bank and home, there was an envelope with a French stamp. I ripped it open and inside was an invitation to become an au pair to Madame Michelle Garcia, in the village of Lons-le-Saunier in the province of Jura. It sounded so romantic, and such a change from a Commer van full of dusty travellers that I could barely contain my glee.

As soon as we reached Gibraltar, I telephoned Madame and we arranged to meet at Dijon station. The tour van dropped me off at Lyon, where I bid my friends adieu, and caught the train to Dijon. The station was full of people, but I must have stuck out like a sore thumb with my battered, dirty suitcase emblazoned with the New

Zealand flag. Madame had no difficulty in spotting me.

'Pardon, are you Meg?' The enquirer was an attractive young Frenchwoman.

'Yes,' I replied, and was consequently showered with kisses on both cheeks as if I were a long-lost friend. We bundled the suitcase and my Moroccan souvenirs into her little 'Deux Chevaux' and swayed off the 100 km into the Jura valley to Lons-le-Saunier. As we drove, Michelle gave me a potted history of her situation.

She was not much older than me, but had fallen in love with and married a dashing young Spaniard three years before. They had two little boys – Robert, aged two and Frederick, aged eight months – but her husband had left her six months ago. He had absconded with much of her inheritance and fled to Spain, leaving her with two babies. Her father, the ex-Mayor, had organised a job for her at the local bank and financed a small house for her. Hence the need for an au pair – she couldn't manage both the job and the children.

'Have you had any experience with children?' she asked.

'No worries,' I lied, fully confident at the age of 20. 'I've looked after heaps of kids at home and have two younger brothers.'

Lons-le-Saunier is a small town (about 7000 inhabitants), set in the foothills of the Jura Mountains. Michelle lived in a small house down a little cul-de-sac on the outskirts of town. There were three bedrooms, a small laundry and a combined kitchen/dining room and lounge. She showed me to a tiny bedroom, barely big enough for a single bed. I unpacked my things, washed three weeks' worth of the Sahara out of my clothes, ate a delicious meal and collapsed, exhausted, into bed.

The following morning, I made friends with the boys. They were cute kids, full of fun and mischief. On the whole it was an easy job; I had to mind the children for five days and was paid F30 (about $3) per week, plus board. Each day, Michelle would leave for work at 8 am. I organised the boys' breakfast, gave them a bath, did the washing and then put them in their pushchair for our morning walk into the village.

Michelle would come home for lunch between noon and 2 pm, and then the boys had an afternoon sleep. I fed the children at

*The village of Lons-le-Saunier.*

about five and Michelle returned at round about seven. I then put the kids to bed and made the evening meal.

Most nights, some of Michelle's friends came round for dinner. I would sit at the edge of the circle, trying to interpret details of affairs, jokes and village gossip with my limited fifth-form French. There seemed to be an extraordinary gulf between the interests of this sophisticated French group and my duties.

The morning walk to the village became an important part of my day. Lons-le-Saunier is a picturesque town, hardly changed from the 16th century. There are old stone houses with brown-tiled roofs. The village square was paved with ancient cobblestones. One end was dominated by the large, Romanesque, stone church; shops encircled the other three sides of the square.

As I walked the boys into the centre of the village on that first morning, the smell of the boulangerie wafted across the square. I took a deep breath, savouring that wonderful, sweet smell of freshly baked bread. I pushed the pram across to the shop window and looked in at a vast array of delicious breads, cakes and pies; brioches and croissants and pastries galore – sprinkled with icing sugar and laced with chocolate, and studded with apples, wild berries, apricot, raisins, flavoured lemon and honey. Oh, wow!

After three weeks of dubious Moroccan cooking, it was almost too good to be true. From the moment I walked through the shop door, I was hooked on pastries. Every morning, I took the boys into the village and we would sample a new delight. I was to put on 3 kg over the next three months, and never regretted a single gram.

It wasn't just the pastries. I was pretty much an oddity in the village – the locals had never met a New Zealander and had no idea where New Zealand was. I never lacked for admirers and was escorted to small wineries, late-night jazz clubs, parties, and restaurants, sampling all that provincial France could offer in the way of food and wine. I learned to ride horses and took fencing lessons, much to the amusement of the class when I misunderstood the instructions and went the wrong way.

I celebrated my 21st birthday there, and my parents organised a large French gateau with candles, together with several bottles of wine and a bottle of whisky. As a treat I had my hair done in the latest French fashion, and had studio photos taken which were duly sent back to New Zealand.

I stayed with Michelle for four months and thoroughly enjoyed life in Jura – their lives, love affairs and most of all the yummy food.

# PAWNING MY PARTNER FOR PETROL

John Smithies always knew he was going to travel; in Invercargill they called it 'voyaging'. After stints in the building trade, he and his wife, Alison, headed for Europe via Canada.

For two years, John worked as a builder around Kent and London; Alison went nursing. In 1966, they bought a Morris Isis and set off home via Iraq, Iran and Afghanistan. Their timing was bad. In August they arrived in Iraq from Jordan just after the 1966 coup that brought the Baathists, and eventually Saddam Hussein, to power. There were roadblocks in every village, and two European travellers in a beat-up Morris Isis were regarded with great suspicion. At one checkpoint, Alison and John were separated for several hours, while inquisitive and suspicious Iraqi army officers attempted an interrogation in broken English. Alison said, 'I didn't feel threatened. It wasn't like an inquisition, but it certainly wasn't comfortable.' There was an underlying assumption that violence was a hair's breadth away.

The Jordanian desert was hot, and unpleasant. Daytime temperatures soared up to 50°C; there were huge, biting flies in the Euphrates valley, humidity was 98 percent, and fungus seemed to appear on clothing and baggage overnight. Baghdad simmered with heat, tension, and incipient violence, so it was with some relief that they left the capital and started the climb towards the Kurdish Mountains along the border with Iran. John continues the story.

By the time we had cleared the checkpoints and crossed the border into Iran, it was late afternoon. Between Kahnaqin and

Kermanshah the road rose in a series of gigantic steps up toward the Iranian plateau. It was little more than a rutted track, following the route of the oil pipeline built by the British between the wars, and we couldn't go more than about 30 kilometres per hour.

The countryside was stony and barren; burnt brown by summer sun and wind. There were few trees save for scraggy thorns; all the forests had been burnt for fuel through centuries of occupation and grazing. Although it was dry there were extraordinary engineered conduits, which carried snowmelt water from the mountains to the cropping land; we were told that some of them were centuries old. The scenery was spectacular, with peaks rising to about 3400 m at Kuh-i-nur.

Kurds lived on both sides of the border and had sided with the Baathists in the early stages of the revolution. And although the villages seemed to be few and far between, as in most parts of the Middle East people appeared from nowhere as soon as we stopped. We'd been warned in the UK that this was bandit country, lawless and wild.

The men wore Kurdish hats, had long moustaches and weather-creased skin. The women were covered from head to toe in black chadors. Alison put her Kiwi shorts away, and wore a long wraparound skirt and a hat, staying as unobtrusive as possible. Throughout the Middle East, European women are conscious that attitudes are different. And although we felt uncomfortable and wary, I don't think we ever felt really threatened; it was just that body language and looks from the men made it quite clear that Alison was of no importance and that her presence was only just tolerable. But on the first day, we were simply pleased to be putting the miles between Iraq and us.

A few kilometres beyond Hamadan, we decided to camp for the night. We found a small stream among some trees and about 30 m from the road. There were no houses in sight, no traffic on the road. It was quiet and apparently deserted, and, for the first time in a week, cool compared with the stinking humidity of the lowlands. We were exhausted after a week of tension and heat, so we put up the tent, cooked a meal and settled down for the night. It was still hot, so we stacked our clothes beside our pillows before lying down to sleep.

That night, we had our best sleep since leaving Jordan 10 days before – until about three the following morning. We woke with a start when a volley of shots rang out. We had a hushed and panicky conversation against a background of sporadic gunfire from the surrounding hills. At first we thought the Iraqi or Iranian army were having a go at the Kurds, then we remembered the bandits. Were they coming to get us? All I had was an old jemmy I used to jack up the car with and that wouldn't have done us any good against armed men. They were probably a gang of smugglers in a shoot-out with the police, but who knows?

We pulled on T-shirts and shorts, bundled up what we could find in the dark, made a quick dash for the car and prepared to leave in a hurry. Although the gunfire soon stopped, we didn't get much sleep. At first light we packed up as quickly as we could and continued on our way, relieved and pleased to be safely away from the alarums of the previous night.

After about three hours' drive, we needed to stop for petrol. There was never a problem finding a petrol pump, even in the remotest part of Iran and Iraq; every 30 kilometres or so there would be a little mud brick hut in the middle of nowhere. Out the front would be an ancient, battered red petrol pump with a wind-up handle – almost as if the pump went straight down into an oil field. We found our petrol station (even tattier than most), drew up, and an old Kurdish man with a huge handlebar moustache shuffled out of the interior and glared at us.

There wasn't a trace of a smile on his face. He was dour and it was plain that he didn't want to have anything to do with these two foreigners except for maybe selling us some petrol. He was on his own, and we could see why.

We got out of the Isis, pointed at the petrol pump and unlocked the cap. He took down the hose, put the nozzle in the filler and slowly, almost reluctantly, began to wind the handle. The glass filled, the meter twirled and after what seemed like an age the gasoline began to flow into the tank.

When the tank was full, I reached into the back pocket of my shorts for my wallet and realised with horror that it wasn't there. When we had settled down in our tent the previous night, the wallet was buttoned into the back pocket of my shorts, which were lying next to my pillow, away from the tent flap; this was part of our security routine. All our other valuable things – passports, traveller's cheques, and papers – were kept in a leather folder, which never left our side. At night, I kept the folder under my sleeping pad. Thankfully, the folder was safe, but all the cash was gone.

I had a sinking feeling in the pit of my stomach and my expression must have been readable in Kurdish, Iraqi and Iranian. While Alison and I anxiously argued about what might have happened to the wallet and what we should do about it, the petrol station owner, ends of moustaches waggling, was becoming more and more animated. He pointed to the Isis, he pointed to the pump, he rattled away in Kurdish at these thieving foreigners and the message was plain.

Traveller's cheques were no good. He glared at them and waved them away with an angry phrase. There were no master cards or

*The Morris Isis in Kurdistan.*

visas in those days. The nearest town was about 30 kilometres back the way we'd come.

But there was nothing else for it. Somehow we managed to convey that I would return to get cash and Alison would stay as a hostage. We decided that would be the safest course of action, rather than the other way round. I don't know who looked more uncomfortable – the Kurdish garage man at the prospect of losing payment for his petrol, or Alison at the prospect of being abandoned on the outskirts of a Kurdish village at the edge of the Iranian plateau as payment for petrol rendered.

The Isis rattled and bounced back to Hamadan in a cloud of dust, faster than was safe on the gravel roads. When I reached the campsite of the night before, I pulled over and ran down to the stream, hoping against hope that I'd dropped the wallet in the vegetation. It was there all right; along with our toilet bag that I'd not noticed was missing in the panic to get into the Isis. But the contents of both were strewn 40 metres away from where we'd pitched the tent and the wallet was empty of cash. The toothpaste tube was just down from the wallet, empty and covered with bite marks. It was clear that someone had crept quietly into the tent during the night while we were asleep, lifted the wallet from my sheets as I slept, and taken the toilet bag for good measure on the way out.

It still gives me the shudders to think about it, but at least we had the traveller's cheques. I raced back to the car and drove on into Hamadan, clashing the gears, working the Isis engine up the slopes and tearing round the corners with my anxiety and imagination running riot.

Where was the bank? No one spoke English. First one street, then another. The one with the big doors, that must be it. It was closed for lunch. Pacing up and down in front of a building and anxious to get back to my wife, I was imagining all sorts of horrible scenarios: bands of mounted smugglers swooping down from the mountains to carry Alison off; an empty hut when I returned. What would I tell Alison's mother?

Eventually, the bank staff reappeared, sauntering along the sidewalk with all the time in the world and unwilling to break the peace of the hot afternoon. First, they slowly turned the key in the door, then they casually opened the grid above the counter. Next they slowly took the traveller's cheque, turning it this way and that, comparing it with the information in their bankbook, suspicious of forgery. Slowly, carefully, filling the forms of currency exchange in time-consuming, anxiety-promoting, meticulous triplicate, while all the time I tried to control my feelings edging close to panic.

Then, with my wallet refilled with Iranian currency, I raced back to the rendezvous, hurtling round the corners again, flying across the potholes and the corrugations.

I needn't have hurried. When I got back, Alison was sitting in the shade of a small tree, reading a book and looking relaxed. The old guy, satisfied that I'd return to collect my wife, had disappeared back inside the hut. And no one else had arrived since my hasty departure – no vehicles, no bands of rapacious tribesmen, nothing exciting at all, she said. Not even, and this was most unusual, a curious child to while away the hours.

The old man reappeared to claim his due. We handed over a wad of money, as well as a generous tip, from relief. Suddenly he was all smiles and so we bowed and he bowed and we smiled and he smiled, and we turned the vehicle and continued on our slow way to Tehran and Afghanistan.

# FEEDING THE BUG

Robyn and Brian Phillips had been acquaintances before they left Wellington, but they weren't travelling partners. Brian travelled to the UK in 1964 with a friend and met an Australian girl, Barbara, on the boat. Robyn had plans to work in Zurich.

However, Robyn's Swiss work permit did not come through, and eventually she was made to leave Switzerland: 'They froze my money in the bank and told me I had to get out in two to three hours. So I jumped on a train and bluffed my way through the customs to London.'

The only person Robyn knew in Britain was Brian's cousin Verna, so she ended up in Verna's flat in Earls Court, along with another girl from Miramar.

In those days there were all sorts of restrictions on moving money around; you couldn't take more than £50 out of the UK, for example, and if you wanted to import a luxury car to New Zealand you had to own it for 21 months.

Brian had an uncle who had been left a tidy bit in the UK, but couldn't get it back to New Zealand. So they hatched a plot that Brian would go to Germany with Verna to buy a Mercedes, spend time in Britain and Europe and then ship the vehicle back to New Zealand. Brian would feed his travel bug, Uncle would get his money from selling the Mercedes and everyone would avoid paying duty everywhere. It wasn't long before we were planning the European tour.

It was an amazing trip: four girls and Brian in an eight-by-eight tent and the Mercedes. It was all very proper. We each had a stretcher – me at one end then Verna, Beverly, Barbara and Brian. At the beginning of the trip, rain or shine, we used to make Brian go outside while we got changed. By the end, he just had to promise to shut his eyes. Washing day was quite a sight. Three pairs of underpants and 40 pairs of knickers.

I was the only other driver but I hated driving. It was a big, heavy car and I could hardly see over the steering wheel, let alone reach the pedals. So I did all the navigation and Brian did the driving. The Mercedes was set up for right-hand drive; if we needed to overtake someone, I'd stick my nose out the window and, if I saw anything coming, yell, 'Quick Brian, get back in!' We had some close shaves on the autobahns.

We went all over Europe, travelling about 160 km a day, and wining and dining at all the local cafés and restaurants. Every time we got to a village, Brian would check out the local pub and whistle us girls in if it looked okay. I don't think we bought a drink in three months. The local lads would queue to buy us a drink and we passed a tithe onto the chaperone. We could eat cheaply in the villages – and almost inevitably we caught the bot.

Now, every traveller gets sick from time to time and most of us recover fairly quickly. All you do is take Gastrolite, Lomotil or Beechams, drink lots of water and sooner or later you'll recover.

But Brian's 'funny tummy' went on and on and he became more and more miserable. The car would come screeching to a halt and Brian would leap out and disappear into the bushes. When we stopped to see the scenery, Brian would go and hide under the rocks to get out of the sun. But he didn't get much sympathy from the others, least of all from Verna who wanted to travel every day.

I vaguely remember my mother telling me that when you got a bad tummy, you soaked bread in raw egg and milk, and that dried you up. So that's what I did. It didn't seem to have any effect though and by the time we got to Rome, Brian had been pretty sick for three weeks. Despite all my bread and milk, he'd lost about 13 kg. The others decided they'd like to stay in Rome for four days, so I said, 'Right Brian, we've got to get you to a doctor.'

We went to the camp office and I tried to tell the concierge that one

*Getting a ticket just outside Genoa (for going through a tunnel without parklights).*

of our party had a sore stomach. I was patting my tummy and trying to mime Brian's predicament in a delicate fashion. As soon as the concierge saw the sign language, she beamed all over her face and launched into an Italian soliloquy that we didn't understand. But it obviously meant that Brian needed the 'Ospedale Gorgonzole' or whatever it was.

She got out an old map and drew a route to the clinic. Brian got into the back seat groaning and moaning, and I set off to find the clinic. I don't know to this day how I ever did it. You know what Rome drivers are like: Fiats and scooters and Alfas and trucks coming at me from all directions, blowing their horns and leaning out the windows, yelling and shouting. It was chaos, so I just closed my eyes and drove through all the intersections. Somehow they all missed me.

Eventually, we found the clinic; a long low building with small windows just off one of the main roads. I drove the Mercedes up to the entrance and Brian half walked, half staggered into the waiting room. It was evidently a hospital monastery of some sort, full of silently moving monks dressed in long brown cassocks. One of them was sitting at a reception desk. He smiled and greeted me in Italian. I said, 'My friend here is sick, we need to do something.'

The reception monk didn't seem to understand, so I went back into mime. Now it isn't easy to mime dysentery delicately, so I rubbed my tummy, pointing at Brian and groaning realistically.

There was dawn of recognition: 'Si. Siete incinta. Un momento. C'è un medico qui e può visitaria.'

What a relief – I was getting somewhere at last. The monk went out the door, and swept back a few seconds later accompanied by two other monks pushing a theatre trolley. Hardly stopping to catch their breath, the two brothers seized my arms, lifted me right off my feet and onto the trolley. They were moving back down into the hospital in an instant, leaving Brian in the waiting room. And through the door I could see a great number of rather large young women in various states of pregnancy.

This was a maternity hospital! They thought I was pregnant. 'Stop! Stop! It's him not me!' I was shouting as I tried to get off the trolley. They began to look extremely puzzled.

'Un momento,' said the first monk and disappeared back into the monastery. A few minutes later, he reappeared with a tall monk, who turned out to be a doctor, and a short, balding monk who had spent some time in America and therefore spoke limited English. Between us, we managed to establish that I wasn't pregnant and that Brian was not a villain, but very sick.

'Da quanto tempo il vostro amico si sente ammalato?' How long has your friend been sick?

'He's got terrible dysentery.' Ha ottenuto terribile la dissenteria. 'I've been feeding him bread and milk but he keeps throwing up.' Sto dandogli il pane ed il latte, ma continua a gettare su.

'Ah,' sighed the doctor monk, shaking his head and looking very serious. Even without translation, I sensed that giving Brian bread and milk had obviously not been the right thing to do.

'State alimentando l'insetto. Ascolta portola a casa niente da mangiare, solo acqua per i tre prossimi giorni, può mangiare un pocho di pane ed aqua, non deve mangiare uovi o latte. Sol aqua a pane asciutto.'

'You've been feeding the bug. Now listen, take him home and he is to eat nothing but boiled water for the next three days, then if he feels like it he can have a little dry bread and water but not milk, no egg and certainly not mixed together.'

So that is what we did: nothing but boiled water for three days. Brian was not a happy person, but once we stopped feeding the bug, he soon came right.

I don't know why, but soon after that incident the order of the stretchers in our tent changed to Verna, Barbara, Beverly, me, then Brian.

# SELLING BLOOD IN ATHENS

Many travellers made money by selling their blood, but it could be a hazardous process. In Greece, if you went to a hospital, you stuck your arm through a hole in the wall and some mysterious, unseen Dracula took your blood and passed back some drachmas. But if you went to the Red Cross, they paid more and you got tea and biscuits.

## SURFIES IN LIBYA

One advantage of travelling by ship is the amount of gear you can take. So when Murray Napier left for Europe in 1965, he took his longboard with him, seizing the opportunity to surf in Ceylon and Aden en route. Jackie followed a few months later by air, and managed to buy a board from another New Zealander in London.

They took a flat in Brighton and were one of the first to try surfing along the south coast – only New Zealanders would be mad enough to surf in English Channel temperatures (17°C in summer). The other tenants in the flat would complain to the landlady: 'You know, those people are bringing boats into the house again.'

This was the era of the Beach Boys and surfing movies – Murray and Jackie saw ENDLESS SUMMER four times in four different countries. So in late 1966, they took the seats out of an old Bedford van, built a bed in the back, put the boards on a roof rack and set off to drive to South Africa and surf Cape St Francis.

Jackie takes up the story.

Loading up the surfboards
in the UK.

We drove down through France and Italy, stopping off from time to time to do the tourist things, although we weren't really into all the museums and churches and that.

The jumping-off point for North Africa was Palermo. From there you took the ferry to Tunis. We intended to drive along the coast through Libya to Egypt and then continue on south to the Sudan and Kenya.

Tunis was warm and friendly; it was also very French, very continental and very exotic. There were the street markets and the souks, with traders selling baked eggs and orange blossom. All the villas seemed to be painted white with blue trim. We stayed for a couple of weeks, then travelled east along the coast road through Carthage and Djerba. Carthage was wonderful; many of the Roman ruins in Tunisia and Libya were in much better shape than many of the more famous sites in Italy.

We arrived in Tripoli in May 1967 and set out to obtain visas for travel to the Sudan. It all took time. Everyone seemed to need six photographs (what did they do with all the mugshots of bored-looking travellers?), 10 forms in triplicate. While we were waiting for the visas and the other documents, we went surfing.

One of the good things about travel is that you meet people you wouldn't ordinarily associate with. Locals and expatriates would talk and socialise because we were Kiwis from overseas. They wanted to know about New Zealand – where we came from, where we were going and what those two funny-looking boats were on the roof of our van. We even bumped into Murray's old English teacher in the supermarket!

We met a young Libyan student who invited us to a party. I just happened to have a cocktail dress in the van; Murray had a shirt and tie (it pays to be prepared for all sorts of things). One thing led to

Beach pass.

another, and before we knew what was going on, Murray had a job with a construction firm and I got work in a kindergarten.

We soon found there were a number of distinct social groups. There was a huge expatriate population of American and Canadian oil workers and engineers who stayed for two or three years, made their money and left. There was the original Italian population. Finally, there was a large American military airbase with several thousand American air force personnel and their families.

Although the Italians and ordinary expatriate workers were more or less part of the country, the airbase was like a piece of Middle America lifted up and dumped in North Africa. Once you'd arrived at the airbase, it was difficult to believe you were on another continent. There were American banks and American shops and American cereals and American TV. Almost all service personnel lived on the base and hardly knew they were in Africa.

There was one other social group that seemed to be isolated from both Libyans and expatriates – a number of European women who were married to Libyan men and whom we met from time to time. They found that being the property of their husbands and having to live with their mother-in-law and all the husband's sisters and aunts

*On a desert road in western Libya.*

was not always easy and many of them were unhappy and felt trapped.

Most of the expatriates lived in the suburb of Giorgimpopoli. We borrowed a house from an English couple; like most other houses in the suburb, it was one storey high and built out of sandstone. On the outside, there was a high wall topped with broken glass to keep out intruders and a high gate. Inside were four bedrooms and two bathrooms.

There were marble and terrazzo tile floors that kept the place cool in the summer, and the walls were of whitewashed plaster, which you could literally hose down. The windows could be shuttered from the outside with Ghibli blinds – roll-down shutters to keep out hot desert sandstorms. There was plenty of Italian furniture. It was all a bit of a luxury for two young surfies from Auckland.

Expatriates had a great social life – oil and engineering firms paid good money, booze was freely available\*, and there were lots of parties. But it wasn't all pleasant. Many of the guys worked weeks at a time out in the desert and many of the relationships didn't last. It was an artificial and very stressed environment.

One month after we arrived, the Six Day War broke out in June 1967. There was a sudden change in the atmosphere of the country and those Americans living off the base seemed to panic; they abandoned their houses, pets and furniture and fled straight on to the base. Within 48 hours, the Americans evacuated all the dependants of the oil workers and service personnel to Greece. It was extraordinary. One guy gave us his furniture and stereo gear – everything.

The other expatriates were more relaxed. Libya didn't get on with Egypt and the Libyan Government suspected that Nasser had designs on the oilfields. Although there was a lot of anti-Israeli and anti-American attitude the government needed the expatriates to run the oilfields. Sometimes it was quite frightening; there were firebombs and riots. One night we heard there was a mob at the

---

\* This was pre Gadaffi.

Egyptian Embassy setting out to march on the infidel. The whole town was put under curfew. Rolls of barbed wire appeared on the highways, there were checkpoints and soldiers toting guns, and rumours and a lot of wild talk. We made sure our van sported a UN symbol and a large picture of Nasser.

But the war to the East didn't stop the socialising. The biggest crisis for some expatriates was when they ran out of tonic for their gin. We'd listen to the BBC and radio and discuss the latest rumours and alarms.

About a week into the crisis we were eating supper one night – I remember we were eating scampi – when there was a sudden bang and a crash and sounds of explosions and people screaming. We were quite sure we were about to be invaded by the mob and lynched.

We shot out of the house to bar the gate, and over the far side of the paddock we could see a glow on the horizon. It wasn't long before the flames subsided and the shouting and the yelling stopped; it turned out to be a cooking fire from a charcoal brazier.

Within a month or so everything was getting back to normal, and the expatriates and oil workers were drifting back wondering what all the fuss was about. We stayed for almost two years, surfing and socialising. But we never did make it to Cape St Francis as the South Africans got snotty over the rugby tour in 1969 and cancelled our visas. We went to Canada instead.

# CAMP COOKING

*Like many other globe-trotters, Judy Appleby didn't have a travel plan – she just went. She caught the* AUSTRALIS *in Auckland and landed in Southampton in February 1969. She worked in a succession of jobs in London and Devon, then booked a tour through Europe with a company called Transit. It was great fun. A year later, Judy booked a six-week trip with Contiki tours through Portugal and Morocco.*

It wasn't a deluxe trip by any means. The company supplied airbeds, tents and a very limited amount of food and equipment. There were a twin burner gas stove, cutlery and plates and a bucket for washing up, but that was it. All the daily chores were shared between the travellers. Everyone would put their own tents up and down, and pairs have a week on cooking duty and help washing up.

The vans themselves carried limited supplies of dried food such as rice and tins of corned beef, but we bought most of our food locally. Each tour had a food kitty – about £10 for six weeks. So each morning, the cooks would be given some of the kitty cash and head into the local market to shop.

You forget how basic the food supply is in remote areas. There were no supermarkets with freezers of shrink-wrapped meat and shop assistants in fancy hats. The meat, piled on bare planks, was as tough as old boots, and probably as old. But you buy what you can get. Sometimes we obtained fresh fruit, vegetables and milk, sometimes there was none. Most of the time we bought the local produce at local prices and didn't think too much about it.

Scrambled eggs for breakfast. Salads and filled rolls for lunch. Stews (a reasonable way of coping with tough meat) and rice for dinner, and if anyone was feeling really creative they might finish with pancakes and fruit for pudding. However, there is a limit to what you can cook when you are catering for 10 people on two gas rings. And if you are hungry, even burnt mince is better than nothing at all.

Besides, if we happened to be at a market round about lunch time, we'd buy two or three shish kebabs for a couple of shillings, a bread roll for three or a chicken and salad for six.

We usually did the washing up in cold water in a plastic bowl. The water would come from a tap, but who knows what supplied the pipe. Inevitably, we'd get sick. My diary notes are punctuated with 'went to bed early', 'so and so has terrible wog', 'spent night running to the loo' and 'mad dash to the bushes'. Looking back I'm amazed at how naïve, in terms of food hygiene, we were.

*The market in Marrakech.*

We had a wonderful time though. I have a lasting souvenir of the trip as well – I met my husband, Stuart, in a bar at the campsite in Madrid.

Pushing the Contiki van in Morocco.

# FISHING FOR BEARS

*In 1969, Dave and Chris Rees set off round Australia in their VW
1500. Breakdowns, floods, heat exhaustion, dysentery and 16,500
km didn't kill the travel bug. In 1971, they set off to tour North
America via the Philippines, Hong Kong and Taiwan, Japan and
Hawaii, landing in San Francisco. They bought a second-hand Ford
Econoline Supervan and fitted it out as a camper, complete with
cupboards and kitchen sink. But by the time they reached Canada
they were running out of money.*

We had heard that you could earn good money in Alaska. Our idea
was that we would go all the way to Alaska to earn a bit of cash and
go back to Canada before winter set in. The van was not well
insulated, and we didn't want to be caught without a job and
accommodation.

We headed northeast out of Vancouver, across the Coastal
Range, then north along Highway 97 towards Prince George and
Damson Creek in the Rockies. This road winds away from the main
route into the Caribo region. There are hundreds of lakes
surrounded by dark, evergreen forests and we glimpsed log cabins
tucked away in the trees.

About seven hours from Vancouver we pulled over at a small
lake just short of a town called Hundred Mile House. There was a
small camping area and one other van on the site. We parked down
by the water and set about cooking some tea whilst it was still
light.

Before long, the campers from the other van, a man and his son,
returned carrying rods and a pair of nice-looking trout. They lit a fire

and soon wonderful smells of woodsmoke and grilled trout started to drift across the campground. The amazing aroma set me salivating – especially after the tinned sardines and beans we'd just eaten.

I used to be an avid fisherman, tramping the Rakaia and the Waimakariri for trout and salmon. The sight of someone else catching and eating fish, and me not sharing the sport, had me bouncing the inside of the van in frustration. As soon as they'd finished eating their dinner and it was polite to do so, we wandered across to the fire and introduced ourselves.

We sat around the embers in the dark while the boy roasted marshmallows, swapping fishing stories and comparing Canada with New Zealand. The father was a fire lookout for a forestry company, but was taking a fortnight's leave for a camping and

**ENJOY THEM AT A DISTANCE**

PARK BEARS AND OTHER ANIMALS ARE **DANGEROUS**

Don't encourage them to approach.

Park regulations prohibit feeding or molesting animals.

Stop cars in pullouts ONLY – not on roadway.

Keep car windows closed when near bears.

THIS WARNING IS FOR YOUR PROTECTION

fishing holiday with his son. He spent most of the fire season perched at the top of a huge tower on the edge of the coastal mountains, scanning for smoke. He got to see all sorts of wildlife as well – moose, caribou, coyote, bears.

'Caribou? Bears?' we asked. That would be exciting. 'I'd like to see a bear,' Chris said.

'Ah, you got to watch out for bears. Run faster than you can – real dustbins. Always on the scavenge for something to eat.'

Talk soon turned to our job-hunting trip to Alaska. 'You don't need to go that far,' he said, poking the fire with a stick. 'There's plenty of work round here, and not enough guys to take it. You could try the mill. And builders are always after summer help.'

We thought that sounded like a pretty good idea. We only had $100 left – barely enough for petrol. Besides, we could camp by the lake and the fishing was obviously good.

Early next morning we set off job hunting. First, we stopped at a sawmill. They would be happy to pay $3 an hour, which didn't sound that much, so we drove on. A few more miles down the road we found a builders' yard. They were looking for a carpenter and would pay $5, but we'd have to come back at 8 pm to see the boss.

That seemed like good money, so we spent the rest of the day exploring the area until the manager came back. His only interest was in whether I could put two pieces of wood together. I took him out and showed him the van.

'Build this yourself?' he asked, peering inside. I was quite proud of the van; we'd bought the shell and I'd fitted cupboards, all the mod cons, everything. He was impressed and offered me a job there and then.

The firm was building log cabins about 20 miles or so from the town. I was to work with two other carpenters, Randy and Pete, building the first log cabin. It was quite a big affair – two-storey, about 180 square metres all up. Although building log cabins is skilled work, it's hardly fine carpentry. Logs are delivered to the site already debarked and oiled. You cut a V notch and a cradle in the end of the log with a chainsaw, then hoist successive logs into position.

Once the walls were in position, we rammed fibreglass wool into the cracks and nailed thick hemp rope on top to cover the glass. By the time we left six weeks later, the roof was on, and most of the deck and fittings were in place.

As we drove back to our lake on the first night, I stopped off at the equivalent of K Mart and bought myself a cheap child's fishing rod. Back at our camp site, Chris settled down in the back of the van to read: 'Do you really think you are going to catch fish with that thing?' she said as I went off along the lake shore with my little rod looking for a rise, feeling like a kid with a new toy.

It can't have been more than a few minutes before I spotted a big rainbow trout cruising the shallows. I cast out the line a couple of metres in front of where I figured the fish was heading, and wound the lure in right across his path. There was a sudden strike, the rod bent double, the cheap reel strained and my heart rate doubled and strained, but the line didn't break. I was soon on my way back to the van with tea for two and a grin fit to bust.

For the next six weeks or so, I fished the lake most mornings and evenings. The weather was fine and warm. We woke up each morning with the mist rising over the lake, dark firs right down to the water's edge and yellow light painting the mountain ranges. The air was crisp, sharp and so clear you'd think you could see a hundred miles ahead. We imagined that this what it must have been like 100 years ago. Most days we ate fish for breakfast, lunch and tea. It was free for the taking and we never got bored with it.

After a cup of tea and some breakfast, we'd set off for work. Randy, Pete and I would chainsaw the logs to size, cutting the cradles and notches, then lifting them into position. Chris did all the light work, stained the decking and so on. About noon she'd stop whatever she was doing and go to the van, set the kettle on for a brew and cook up trout for lunch. You could always tell when lunch was on the go, because this wonderful smell would drift into the cabin and there was no question of any further work until we'd eaten.

Late one morning, about two weeks into the job, Chris went to the van to start lunch – trout as usual – and before long we could smell the fish cooking. We stopped the chainsaws and were getting ready to move outside into the sun, when Chris suddenly screamed, 'There's a bear, there's a bear! Quick, quick there's a bear!'

A mad scamper out of the cabin followed. Just across the clearing were two brown bears, over a metre tall, investigating the van. Back in New Zealand you sit in an armchair and look at wildlife pictures of bears and they look all cuddly. But these were big beasts, quite big enough to do an awful lot of damage. They had smelt lunch and liked the menu.

There was a tremendous scramble and lots more yelling and shouting. Randy was yelling, 'Close the doors!', Pete started up a chainsaw and Chris slammed the doors. Even armed with a chainsaw apiece, we didn't feel we were much of a match for two big bears. Luckily for us, they didn't like the noise and soon disappeared into the woods.

Later, Chris wrote in her diary, 'Scared the hell out of me.' Scared the hell out of me too. We kept a sharp lookout after that and closed the van doors whenever we were cooking fish.

*Dave and Chris at their campsite by the lake.*

# THE MOST IMPORTANT MAN IN TOWN

*In 1968, Rod Wilson and two English travellers had spent a week on the Nile Ferry and were hitching north through the Sudan.*

At the first village we came to, the driver told us to check in at the police station. Although we didn't really want to, we dutifully went to the dusty old building in the central village. The police had uniforms and rifles, and you did what you were told.

The policeman was a pleasant enough fellow and after a few moments' conversation, offered us a bed in the cells.

*Rod on a watermelon truck near Senegal.*

'You're not going to lock the door, are you?' we asked.

'Ah no, no, but you'll be better off in there than in a ditch outside.'

We could see some empty cells in the back, and we thought that was a great idea. Better still, when we got up the next day, the police chief asked, 'Where are you going now?'

We got out the map and pointed out the next village. He said, 'I'll stop a truck for you.' And he did – flagging down the first truck to arrive and telling the driver to take us where we wanted to go.

We quickly realised the police chief was the best person in the village to know. For the next week we had a great system; as soon as we got to a village we'd head for the police station and ask if they had any free cells. Sometimes they did and sometimes they didn't.

We even slept in the police barracks, but that wasn't exactly comfortable: bugle calls and drill at five in the morning. Criminals were quieter.

# GROSSLY OVERLOADED

Rod Wilson boarded the ACHILLE LAURO to Sydney in 1966 to get to a motor scooter rally near Bathurst. After a year in Australia, he continued on to Durban, then travelled overland to Cairo. In 1971, Rod took a job as a tour driver for a company called Atrek Travel.

*Rod (top right) and the group on the overloaded van.*

None of the travel companies was exactly flash. Most of the drivers were travellers like myself – Australians, New Zealanders, South Africans, all out for a big adventure.

Touring with a company like Atrek wasn't an expensive way to go. Our 11-week trip through 16 countries cost $NZ526 plus $79 for the food kitty and $11 for visas. You took your spending money on top of that, making a bit on the side by smuggling US dollars into the East to change on the black market. We made quite a good profit as the official rate in the Soviet Union was two roubles to the dollar and we could get five times that on the black market.

Atrek used six-wheeler Ford Transit vans; they had a bench seat across the front and four rows of bench seats behind. We packed 15 people into the vans, mountains of food under the seats and all the tents, pots, pans, stoves and rucksacks flung up on a huge roof rack until the springs groaned under the load.

The vans were grossly overloaded. This was fine in Western Europe, where there are smooth tarmac roads and garages in every town, but such luxuries became less and less frequent the further east we went.

The fun began almost as soon as we crossed the Iron Curtain into Eastern Europe. Bulgarian guards spent an hour examining documents; Rumanian officials were more thorough and took two. But the Soviet guards at the Ukrainian border really knew how to make a tour group feel welcome.

First, one of the guards collected all the passports and took them into a back room for a couple of hours. I think they phoned the details of every passport through to Moscow for clearance.

Other guards checked the van. Everything had to come off the roof rack – the tents, the bags, the cooking gear. Everything had to come out from inside the van – the food, the games, the books. We stacked everything by the side of the road. All the bags were opened and the toothpaste sniffed and tasted. All the cameras were turned this way and that, and passed from guard to guard. All the girls' beauty gear was admired in meticulous detail.

Meanwhile, yet another detachment of guards took the panels off the van. They brought out little dentists' mirrors on sticks to look under the chassis, into the engine, and behind the spare wheel. For six hours, 15 Western travellers sat by the side of the road, playing cards and listening to Beatles tapes, whilst the defenders of the State looked for goodness only knows what. We were the first European tour bus to enter the Soviet Union by this route and we probably made their day.

Once we'd finally got our clearance from Moscow or wherever, everything had to be reloaded and on we'd go, with the *Intourist* guide squashed in the front.

The guide's job was to make sure we followed a set route and to report back to his bosses at regular intervals. We weren't allowed to deviate: we had to reach set points every day and as we passed the control boxes, we could see the guards lift the telephone and phone ahead to the next. We could be fined if we were late*.

Our aim was to cover about 400 km a day and spend longer in big cities like Moscow and Leningrad. In theory, we could drive that distance without too much trouble. In practice, it was just about impossible. Thirty kilometres across the border the roads got rougher, the average speeds slower and long days longer. Sometimes the roads were sealed for short distances; most times they were dirt. We bounced in and out of potholes and steered round gravel patches and mud holes. On occasions, the entire group would have to get out and walk or push the van through the mud.

Although the vans were relatively new, they weren't exactly Rolls Royces. One of the main bearings failed in Istanbul. The battery packed in between Moscow and Leningrad. The vans were fitted with (tubeless) retreads that weren't designed for rough gravel and corrugated clay. It wasn't long before the treads began to lift and the tyres to blow. The first puncture was in Kiev, the second in Kharkov. We had two for the price of one outside Moscow.

As we only carried one spare tyre, I began to worry that we'd never get back to the West. But once past the border everyone, even the officials, were incredibly friendly and helpful. The police would

---

* Actually Russian cops could fine you for anything, including £8 for having a dirty van.

flag down passing motorists to see if they had a spare (none did – Ford transit tyres were quite a different size from the Russian standard). One policeman took us to a tractor factory in Kiev where they tried to vulcanise a truck inner down to size. Another officer helped pump our tyres with the hand pump off his motorcycle, sweating in the heat of the Russian summer.

The electrics died in Leningrad and the van would go no further. I sent my party on by train and arranged a tow from a Russian truck. Sixteen kilometres from the Finnish border, the driver stopped, undid the tow rope, and turned round. He was allowed to go no further. I waited for a day until a second Atrek van arrived and towed me into the West. We stopped at the first garage in Finland to fit three new tyres, a battery and service the engine until it was fit to drive back to London. I don't think Atrek made much profit from that first tour.

# MUTINY ON THE *GALILEO*

*Linda Dakin grew up in Invercargill and Oamaru. After a year teaching in Whakatane, she set off for Britain on a Lloyd Triestino liner, the* GALILEO GALILEI, *in 1976.*

Quite by chance, I ended up sharing a cabin with two girls I'd known from school. I hadn't seen Elaine and Robyn since school days, but it was a relief to have familiar faces around for the first part of the journey. There were others I vaguely knew from South Canterbury, a middle-aged couple from Oamaru, and one or two people from Christchurch.

We left Auckland in March, the ship steaming north to Noumea, then west to Tahiti. We soon got into a shipboard routine: lounging by the pool during the day, getting changed for dinner, dancing each night or watching a movie. We took Italian lessons and read books. In truth, I remember very little. What I do remember is that the first part of the journey was pleasant, undemanding and cheerful.

We stopped off at Noumea, where I bought a camera; and in Tahiti where we hired horse-drawn buggies for a trip around the capital. We celebrated crossing the line in 'traditional style'; the crew laid on a ceremony where King Neptune sentenced various members of passengers and crew to dunkings or other indignities.

But it wasn't all plain sailing and there was an undercurrent of dissatisfaction and discontent. Several of the older passengers had paid for a world tour and they weren't at all satisfied with the standard of accommodation, food or organisation, while the younger women were constantly pestered by the crew. After our stopover in Tahiti, the ship was supposed to head for Acapulco before cruising on through the Panama Canal to Curaçao in the Dutch Antilles. Acapulco had a fine reputation, and we were all looking forward to a full day off ship.

Somewhere in the middle of the Pacific, the *Galileo* received a distress call from an oil tanker – a crewman on board was severely injured and needed urgent treatment. The *Galileo* had a doctor and a reasonable ship's hospital, so the captain diverted the liner to take off the injured man.

We reached the oil tanker at about 1 am on Monday. Most of the passengers and crew lined the deck as the tanker and the liner steamed slowly, about half a kilometre apart, separated by calm waters. The gap between the vessels was lit by powerful lights: an eerie circle within a well of darkness. We watched as the tanker lowered a lifeboat, which then motored across to the *Galileo*. The injured man, strapped to a stretcher, was winched on board, the ships hooted a salute, the lights went off and everybody retired to our cabins.

The following morning, the rescue felt rather unreal, like an

The GALILEO GALILEI.

episode from a movie. The oil tanker was gone, the ocean empty of ships – a momentary diversion from the ordinary routine of the cruise. But it had been real enough. The diversion and delay meant that the liner would not reach Acapulco until 7 pm on Wednesday. The captain announced that the *Galileo* would still leave at 3 am on Thursday, presumably in order to get to the Panama Canal on schedule. All the passengers were to be back on board by 2 am at the latest. The implication was that otherwise they would be left behind.

For some of the passengers this was a major blow. Acapulco was supposed to be a highlight of their tour. There were the cliff divers and the markets and Marachis and just the opportunity to be back on land and eating something other than pasta. (The novelty of voyaging soon fades after three weeks at sea.)

Several of the passengers, led by a German baron called Joachim and vociferously supported by older English and American passengers, began to agitate for a change in schedule to allow them a full day on shore.

Joachim was a striking and distinguished-looking man of about 30 years of age. He was tall and gaunt, much as I imagined a German baron should be, but he was no diplomat. His petition threatened to inform the news media of all of Lloyd Triestino's shortcomings. He would start a hunger strike, mount a campaign against the food and blacken the company's name in Europe and the USA.

Nor was the captain willing to compromise, so tempers frayed, fists were shaken and the baron tried to tear off the second-in-command's epaulettes. Rumours and counter-rumours passed from passenger to passenger. By Wednesday night, you could feel the tension in the atmosphere. The older passengers were simmering with anger and the crew were sulky and unhelpful.

We must have arrived in Acapulco at about seven in the evening. There was no dock, and the passengers were ferried to shore in the ship's launches. It was late by the time we arrived and again, the purser had given strict instructions that all passengers were to return by 2 am.

Acapulco was not about to miss the opportunity to trade. All the hawkers were curled up on the pavement fast asleep, waiting for the customers to disembark. They awoke to sell their wares: bark paintings and cheap rings, onyx chessmen and Aztec souvenirs. Our small group had a wonderful three hours wandering the markets and bartering for goods.

About midnight, we met Ingrid, Joachim's partner. She was distraught: Joachim had been thrown off the ship. The crew had threatened to beat him up and she didn't know where he was. We hurried back to the launches, concerned to find out what was going on.

The launch crews were now rude and aggressive, their whole attitude and demeanour threatening and rough. They made no effort to help the older passengers on board, but talked loudly to each other in Italian. We climbed the steps and made our way up into the lobby.

One end was packed with passengers talking angrily amongst themselves: 'How dare they treat us like this. We've paid for our cruise. This is ridiculous!' At the other end were the crew, glaring at the passengers and muttering amongst themselves. Around the sides of the lobby were groups of Mexican police in blue uniforms, tapping truncheons in their hands and fingering their holsters. The atmosphere simmered with resentment, anger and threat.

At about three in the morning, the police left. Without any warning, the crew charged the length of the lobby, laying into the passengers with fists and feet. There were screams and yells. Several of the crew grabbed the fire hoses, turning the jets on the men and women, driving them down the passageway. Robyn and I made it to our cabin and stood there shaking, angry and frightened. We stayed in the cabins for the rest of the night, listening to the sound of the engines getting under way, hating the ship and the crew, just wishing we were in Europe and away from the mess.

The following morning we were told that Joachim, Ingrid and the other ringleaders of the petition had been beaten up and removed from the ship by the Mexican police. There was never any apology from the ship or the line. The crew stayed surly, alternately avoiding people's eyes or looking smug, as if to say, 'You had better stay in line or else . . .'

The next few days were awkward and strained, but it was surprising how quickly the events in Acapulco were forgotten. There were new and different sights to enjoy: the Panama Canal, Curaçao, Malaga and Messina. However, we never found out what happened to the mutineers.

# AT NUWEIBA

Sara Kay went on her OE from 1971 to 1978, starting in Australia before 'doing the overland' to the UK. She spent time in England in a squat,* then headed to Saudi Arabia as a nanny for a Saudi Arabian princess living in a harem in the king's palace. Much of the time the family lived it up on oil money in pre-war Lebanon and Europe. They stayed in the best hotels and ate at the finest restaurants. In 1975, Sara left Saudi Arabia and briefly returned to London, before venturing to Israel to work on a kibbutz.

Sarah's hut at Nuweiba.

---

\* Squatting was taking over and living in an empty house, often as part of a commune.

One long weekend, the other volunteers and I went to Nuweiba for a camping holiday. There was a hippy community just south of the main camp site. It was so beautiful, I couldn't bear to leave.

Nuweiba means 'place of the spring'. It is on the Red Sea, about 60 kilometres south of Elat, where the Sinai Desert meets the Red Sea. You can look across the Khalig al Aqaba to the rocky mountains of the Saudi peninsula shimmering in the haze. The colours change all the time and the sea glistens like a magic mirror. But the land is harsh and desolate; away from the spring, there is little vegetation: sand and hard rocks, punctuated with spindly, struggling bushes. Everything is raw and elemental, and reduced to the bare essentials.

There were three distinct communities at Nuweiba. First, there were the Israelis at the moshav. A moshav is like a kibbutz except that people own their own plots, but they share major facilities like the packing house and the quarters. There were about a hundred Israelis, growing melons and peppers for the winter market in Europe. They also ran a kiosk and a beach resort.

Then, just south of the moshav, there were about fifty hippies, mainly from Europe. They weren't a permanent community; people came and went the entire time, staying a week, quite out of it on drugs. They slept it off in the sand dunes, drifting in and out of consciousness, then disappeared back to Europe.

We lived a separate life, 4 kilometres or so down the beach. We were a permanent community, living in five houses, each separated by a goodly walk in between. Most of us were single: a Frenchman, two Germans, a Swiss guy, a Scottish girl and a girl from Brazil. Then there was a family with a baby. We ate together frequently but mostly did our own thing for the rest of the time.

The houses were huts made of driftwood, sheets and blankets, old bits of packing case and plastic bags. My house had been built by an aircraft engineer from California. It was a relatively sophisticated contraption of canvas and driftwood, with wind-down blinds where the mice used to run. But snakes would come and hunt the mice and they'd make an awful noise.

I had a dog called Doga and two cats called Ahava and Hiya,

which is Hebrew for 'love' and 'life'; typical hippy names for animals.

Our only need was to find food and water, literally life's bare necessities. There was no pressure to consume, meet deadlines, or conform with others' needs. We were suspended in an envelope of peace and calm. After the frenetic pace of London and the pressures of the Hulda kibbutz, it was glorious.

We cooked over an open fire and slept in the open. Food came from all sorts of places. I spoke fluent Arabic and I think this pleased the local Arabs. I could buy goats' milk from the Bedouin women. At night, some of the hippies would sneak off and steal water and vegetables from the moshav. I'm sure the moshav knew about it.

Then there was a Bedouin truck that used to come in from Elat on Saturdays, the Hebrew Sabbath. So every Saturday morning, an old Arab guy used to come by my hut. He would order his camel down so that I could climb up and off we'd ride, making small talk in Arabic. He would take me to the Bedouin truck, where I'd buy supplies and then walk back home.

Most of the time we were naked, wearing no clothes at all. You could see for miles and we kept a sarong close by in case someone came along. Most of the local population, Bedouin and Israelis, were very relaxed. They didn't really like us being there, but they tolerated the odd people in their midst, though the police kept a close eye on the druggies. In fact, the beach warden would come down the beach from time to time to check that everyone in the community was in good health.

It was just as well. I couldn't have been eating all that well as I used to give most of my meat to my animals, so I eventually developed vitamin A deficiency. Over about 10 days my whole body erupted into boils and it took me an hour to turn over in bed. Needless to say I didn't have the strength to go look for help. I also couldn't stand bright light and thought I was going to die alone in my little hut.

And I might have done, I suppose, but the beach warden came down on one of his regular checks and found me. He called in the local police and the moshav doctor promptly gave me a jab in the bottom. It was amazing how quickly it worked, but it was obviously time to leave.

I didn't really want to come home, but I'd overstayed my welcome and my visa wasn't going to be renewed. I arrived back in Auckland dressed in a Bedouin costume – what a shock to my poor parents.

## INSECT BITES

In the late 1960s, the Virgin Isles were duty free. Vodka was so cheap that people used it to clean their windows. It was also good for insect bites, and you could lick your wounds.

# BATS IN THE DRAKENSBERG

In 1972, Nigel McCarter volunteered for the International Voluntary Service. He thought he was going fish farming in Latin America, but IVS sent him teaching in Botswana. At this time, there were about 75 British volunteers and a greater number of Peace Corps, Canadians and Scandinavians scattered between Botswana, Lesotho and Swaziland. Most of them were assigned to mission schools and used the holidays to explore Southern Africa. During one holiday, Nigel met up with a group of other volunteers in Lesotho and they decided to spend a day bat hunting in the Drakensberg Mountains.

In the canyon looking for crabs.

Lesotho is a tiny, landlocked country surrounded entirely by South Africa. It spans an area of about 30,000 square kilometres, about the size of Waikato and Bay of Plenty together; in the east, the Drakensberg Mountains rise to almost 3500 metres. Lesotho was, and still is, one of the poorest nations in Africa.

Although the country was officially 80 percent Christian, in practice, Western culture was a veneer of convenience. In the villages, the customs and rules governing all aspects of life – how to punish thieves, when to plant crops, who should marry whom and how to settle a dispute – were entirely Basotho*.

Most volunteers, teachers, agronomists and engineers were well aware that they were also a part of a veneer – brief shadows in the African light who were there for two years to do what they could and then return to their own countries and lives.

On this occasion, I'd arranged to meet other volunteers in Maseru during the August holidays. Maseru in the 1970s was not much bigger than a small New Zealand town, say Feilding or Rangiora, so I soon found the others and we repaired to one of the volunteer houses to drink beer, swap yarns and make plans.

There were 14 of us: IVS from Britain, Peace Corps from America and a Canadian and a Swede. We draped ourselves around a sparsely furnished room, sipping beer, chatting and strumming guitars. Outside one could hear the tinkling of goat bells and the rumbling, resonant cadence of an unfamiliar language, smell the cattle and smoke of cooking fires and wonder at the noises of the African bush. Inside, it could have been any student flat from the 1960s through to the present.

Liz was working in a Catholic mission station in the ranges, six hours' drive from Maseru across the God Help Me Pass. Jenny taught at a state school in Botswana. Alastair worked on a food aid programme. Rose was a Peace Corps agronomist, and so on.

Sue and Chris had come down from Pitseng in the mountains

---

* In the Sotho group of languages, qualifiers come at the beginning of nouns. So Botswana and Lesotho are countries, Batswana and Basotho are the citizens, and Setswana and Sotho are the languages.

two weeks early – their mission station had closed rather mysteriously. 'Most of the kids have gone off to initiation school,' they told us glumly, and we all shuddered slightly.

There was a great deal of rumour and discussion about initiation schools. Throughout Africa, initiation ceremonies, staged when boys and girls reached puberty, were common. In Lesotho boys would be taken to a secret place somewhere in the bush and instructed in the culture and rites of the tribe.

We'd been told that the initiation ceremonies for the Basotho required the boys to undertake some kind of ritual trial. We weren't clear as to what form the trial took, but assumed it would prove manhood through pain or endurance. It was known that the initiation school culminated in ceremonial circumcision. When circumcised, the boys would be accepted into the tribe as men.

The schools were a crucial part of Basotho culture. But for years, missionaries throughout Africa have tried, usually without success, to stamp out the initiation practice. They view circumcision and initiation as a heathen and dangerously subversive practice. Who is subverting who depends entirely on one's point of view of course; and the tribal elders' view of mission stations is not recorded.

But dangerous it certainly was. Adult circumcision is risky at the best of times; when performed by tribal elders with sharp flints or rusty knives, septicaemia and death were inevitable for a proportion of the boys.

Missionary endeavours to suppress the schools had an unintended consequence. Initiation schools were secret, both to keep the school away from the authorities and to amplify tribal identification: this is ours, no one else can share our secret knowledge. Boys would simply disappear from mission stations and return the following term as men, if they returned at all.

It was widely rumoured amongst the European community that should a non-tribal person stumble across a school, they would be killed to preserve and protect sacred tribal lore. Alternatively, one could be pressed to join the ceremonies – not a particularly attractive option given the surgery at the end of training. Sandy scoffed and said he'd run into three initiation schools whilst walking in the mountains, and although he still had everything he came with, he had certainly felt threatened and it had been made very clear to him that he wasn't welcome.

The conversation swung between the inevitable trite jokes and an earnest attempt to grapple with the ideas. None of us would enter a mosque without removing our shoes, nor interrupt a mass with coarse behaviour. If the Basotho wished to keep their sacred ceremonies a secret, who were we to condemn?

The conversation went round and round until late into the night and without conclusion. Eventually the topic died from exhaustion and we switched to planning activities for the holidays.

Alastair had found an old *National Geographic* featuring bats of the world. He had heard that one could find African bats in a valley near Khabos, between Butha-Buthe and Leribe. It seemed like a good idea, so we decided we'd take a picnic and go bat hunting in the foothills of the Drakensberg the following day.

Early the next morning, we overloaded a long-wheel-base land rover and a ute, and headed for Khabos along a dirt road. The countryside was poor and barren, punctuated by small villages of a dozen or so rondavels. Most families built two rondavels; they cooked in one and slept in the other. The rondavels were linked by small walls, incised with intricate designs and decorations, that enclosed a courtyard. Larger stock areas were fenced by telegraph-pole aloes – the flower spike poking three or four metres above a thick hedge of succulent leaves. There were scraggly sheep, mohair goats and potbellied Basotho ponies.

Around the villages, people had planted peach trees and the pink and white blossom was a welcome counterpoint to the brown veld. There were a few small, unfenced fields growing crops of sorghum and mealie maize. But the plants were struggling in the dry, poor soil; most food was imported from the mechanised farms of the Orange Free State and the Transvaal.

Closer to the mountains, the foothills terminate abruptly in 100-metre cliffs, rather like the sandstone scarp at Katoomba in New South Wales. Deep valleys cut into the cliffs and we were making for one of these. Where the strata overhung the valley floor, there were caves deep enough to house bats. There were no trees, but low shrubs, thorn bush, coarse grass and a heather-like plant.

We forded a small river, parked the vehicles and unloaded paraffin lamps and candles for the cave. It didn't seem appropriate to be carrying lights in the bright sunlight, but as we walked up the valley, the walls began to encroach and the light faded.

The cave was supposed to be about halfway up on the western side below a rock formation we nicknamed the garage doors. This was a sheer slab of rock, split down the middle by a vertical crevasse. The whole formation looked like the entrance to a giant's abode.

It was a fairly steep climb and at high altitude. After a couple of kilometres, we stopped to regain our breath. As we sat quietly, we could hear the most peculiar sound, like a cross between an out-of-tune organ and wind whistling in the rocks. We turned our heads this way and that, trying to locate the source of the sound.

Ten minutes later we continued to climb. About 400 metres further on, we must have all come to a collective realisation, and were brought up short in horror. It wasn't the wind whistling in the rocks. It was chanting. We had run into an initiation school.

Right on cue, out of the scrub rose about a half a dozen Basotho, shouting and waving with anger. Each carried a small ceremonial shield and two sticks, brightly decorated with beads and paint. These were the guards to an initiation school and they were not at all pleased to see us. After the previous night's conversation we felt apprehensive and uncomfortable.

Chris spoke Sotho. When the initial surprise to both parties wore off, there was a lengthy conversation in words and mime. It became clear that we weren't allowed forward nor to turn back. The upshot was that we were escorted off the track and guided up to a cave with a specific instruction that we were to stay for one hour, then leave by a set route. School was due out at about 1 pm and an audience would not be welcome.

We complied, but not before finding our bats. The cave itself sloped downwards at an angle of about 45 degrees into a deep, recessed overhang. It was over 20 metres deep and 40 metres wide and the bats hung like fat grapes from the ceiling. Where the roof closed to the floor, we could stand and ease them from their roost to be measured and examined. Delightful little creatures – though not everyone was enthused. The thought of little mice with sharp teeth and wings was too much for one or two of our group, so they sat outside on point duty. But we didn't stay long. Somehow the notion of bat hunting had rather lost its attraction.

By the time we emerged from the cave, the guards had disappeared and the chanting had stopped. We started down the gorge again as rapidly as we could, not wishing to cause offence. When we reached a point where we could look over the plain below the scarp, we could see streams of people walking towards the valley mouth. They were coming to welcome the newly celebrated men. None of us cherished the idea of remaining in the area, so we drove a few miles upstream until we we were well away from the ceremonies.

We sat in a circle below a group of green willows, passing crisps and sausages and tearing hunks of bread and fruitcake laced with brandy; drinking Spelleta and telling jokes and stories. We fed orange peel to the goats and hunted in the stream for freshwater crabs and toad spawn and pretty stones for Sue's mum in New York. We talked about the students jailed in Fiksburg for crossing the border illegally, and about the barbed wire round the townships. We built sandcastles and made mud pies, forgetting, for a moment, that we were in Africa.

# POLICE STATIONERY

*Judy and Margaret Kane were from Te Kuiti. They arrived in Britain in 1973 and, after a succession of jobs, started off on their European Tour.*

Margaret and I decided to take the train from Milan to Venice. We were talking to another traveller at the station, when we were jostled by a group of guys. We didn't think anything of it at the time. It was a crowded station and Italian guys take any excuse. They can be charming, they can be courteous, they can pour on the compliments like cream into coffee. Sometimes it was amusing, mostly it was irritating. So we would just glare at them, 'Non comprende' or rather 'comprende' only too well, and they would usually disappear.

In Italy, they checked the tickets on board the train. There was no barrier or ticket collector and you had your ticket clipped at some point in the journey. So we made our way on to the platform, got on the train and settled down, making ourselves comfortable for the 250 kilometre trip.

Before long the conductor arrived to check our tickets. Margaret pulled her bag down from the rack, opened the wallet and went grey. Everything was gone – her passport, her wallet, the tickets, everything of value. The amorous guys at the station must have been a team of pickpockets. They had rifled through her bag while we were standing talking on the platform.

The conductor did not look as if he believed us. We spoke no Italian, and he spoke no English. But eventually, between us and the other travellers, we managed to explain that we had bought the tickets, but they had been stolen. The conductor muttered under his breath but allowed us to stay on the train.

We arrived in Venice in the early afternoon and decided that the first thing to do was to report the theft to the police. There was a small police post next to the railway station and so in we went.

Inside there was a small reception counter and three uniformed garda sitting around a wooden table. They weren't much older than us, and didn't look as if they had much to do. The garda wearing the most braid got up and came to the reception counter. Once more we went through a pantomime explaining that our passports and money had been stolen.

He listened attentively, asking questions in passable English. After a few minutes' discussion he said: 'We will have to write an official report.' Pointing at Margaret, he said, '. . . and you must stay here in the police house.' Then, bowing to me, he added: 'You must come with me to get the report form.' Then all the other garda nodded solemnly in agreement.

Margaret asked, 'Where do you get the forms? Why can't I come too?'

'Ah,' he replied, 'if visitors to Italy lose your passport you have to purchase special reports from stationery shop.'

It wasn't what we would do in New Zealand, but we were in Italy and it didn't sound completely barmy. So Margaret sat down with the other two garda and I set off with Guilo, or whatever his name was, to purchase the official missing passport form from the stationery shop.

He talked non-stop, looking elegant in his uniform and braid, charming and expansive. We couldn't have walked far, but I was soon well and truly lost. We turned a corner, and on the far side of the square was a small shop. Guilo put his hand to his forehead with a theatrical gesture: 'Mama mia, I forgot, siesta time. Two hours we have to come back. Never mind, I show you Venice.'

I was appalled. 'What about my sister?'

'No, no, no, no, she'll be fine. My friends they look after her.'

There didn't seem to be much I could do, so off we went for the little tour. The station was not in the centre of town, and we didn't visit St Mark's Square. Instead, he showed me his favourite bar, he introduced me to his friends, showed me the house of his ex-wife, took me to drink coffee and eat pastry at his favourite café and finally, after two hours, he took me back to the stationery shop.

It was now open. I bought a pad of the official forms and we returned to the police station. Margaret was sitting looking bored in the company of the two garda, attempting stilted conversation in broken English. We duly filled in the forms in triplicate, noting the place of the theft and the passport number. The forms were signed, dated and stamped and then we all smiled, said our goodbyes and Margaret and I made our way to the hostel.

Later, in Rome, we went to the embassy to get another passport. 'Tell me,' I asked the clerk, 'does Italian law have an official report form for a lost passport?'

'Oh, I don't think so,' she said. 'Usually people just come straight here, we ask a few questions, check their passport numbers and give them a replacement.'

Simple, really.

*Judy with her Italian 'hosts'.*

# CAST EWES AND MUTTON BONES

John Cousins is a third-generation New Zealander who grew up on, and still farms, the family farm near Feilding. With two older brothers and a sister, one member of the family was always travelling. In 1976, John took his turn. His journey took him through the USA and Canada to London, where he bought a van – an old Commer with a column change, which led to a few close calls – and eventually ended up on the island of Iona, off the Scottish coast.

Jimmy was a crofter on Iona; he was the ferryman, the local odd job man for the laird, the fixer and a man of very few words. He owned three crofts and ran 80 or so sheep and a few cattle of indeterminate breed on their land holding. He rented out the surplus crofts in summer, but the living was mean.

Jimmy shearing a sheep.

He must have been 48 or 50 years old, weather-beaten face, clean-shaven, always in holey trousers held up by string, Wellington boots and a rough jumper. Good working gear. He lived in one of the crofts with a cheerful, rotund wife; I couldn't understand one word of what she said, her accent was so broad. He only spoke English when he wanted me to understand. At meal times he and his wife would carry on a conversation without me comprehending a thing.

I ended up working for him by pure chance. I was walking near Jimmy's land and found a cast ewe. The land was all run down; the walls and gates in need of repair. When you are travelling, you always keep half an eye open for the chance of a job and a bit of a change, so coming from a farming family, I set the ewe to rights, then wandered over to the nearest croft to pass the time of day and report the beast.

Somehow, I landed bed, meals and money for 'a short time and weel see what weel make o ye'. I helped Jimmy with a variety of jobs: mowing the lawns for the laird, Mr McKenzie (my introduction to whisky), general farming maintenance (which I was well used to) and building a concrete wall at one of the crofts. He was putting on an additional room, because the rental business was quite a profitable exercise.

The accepted method of building was to construct a wide concrete wall and fill it in with boulders and rocks from the beach. So we'd take an old Ferguson tractor down to the beach and shovel sand and gravel into the trailer for the concrete. The tractor was rusty and dilapidated, virtually rusted away. It was a two-person job to start it, so one of us would sit on the tractor, while the other held a screwdriver across the terminals. We didn't dare stop on the beach for fear we'd never get it started again.

We'd build the boxing, turn the cement in the barrow, wheel it up a bendy six by two plank and tip the mix in at the top of a 2-metre-high wall. Then we'd tamp down boulders and stones. I was used to a 1:5 cement to builder's mix; on Iona they used 1:12, but the houses have lasted for centuries. As the wall grew higher, Jimmy would stand up on top with a fishing gaff and haul on the wheel until, inevitably, the barrow toppled and spilt.

We'd also take the tractor down to the hotel to collect the scraps. We brought these back to the croft and it was a bit of a mystery what Jimmy and his wife did with them. There were no pigs and the remains went out again the following day into a pit.

I stayed in one of the crofts with an elderly woman, Sarah, who I think was a relative of Jimmy's. She was stone deaf and didn't seem to speak English. She lived in a spartan house with wooden floors, which was cold, even in summer. We had porridge for breakfast (of course) and a fill of potatoes for supper. I'd take a midday feed with Jimmy, which was always broth.

The broth simmered in a big pot on the stove and basically consisted of the soup of the day before, with a handful of lentils and usually a bone or two with a smidgin of meat on them.

One morning, I remember visiting the hotel and noting some substantial bones amongst the scraps. Jimmy and I went off to repair gates on some section of the land and returned as usual at about midday. We'd been talking about stock prices and farming in New Zealand and Scotland, and I remember asking, 'Do you ever eat sheep meat, Jimmy?'

'Oh no no,' was the reply. 'They're too valuable for that.'

Jimmy's wife brought the usual bowl of broth, with thick slabs of bread. Floating in the soup pot were the same bones I'd collected from the hotel that morning.

I looked at the bones, and I looked at the bucket. If the sheep were worth too much to slaughter, the scraps from the rusty bucket were going to the dogs via our soup. Well cooked they might have been, but my appetite wasn't that keen.

The following day we finished the wall, setting in notches for the roof joists. The job complete, it seemed like a suitable point to move on. Besides, after six weeks of porridge and soup, I was beginning to crave a more substantial feed, and of more certain provenance. I made my farewells and climbed into the Commer to drive back to London.

Jimmy's last comment was: 'Weel ye're no bad at concrete, but ye'll niver make a farmer.'

# RENAISSANCE

*Libby Newton was born and raised in Ashburton and grew up expecting to 'travel the world'. She left home in 1970, travelled through Africa to Europe and returned home in 1971. In 1972 Libby set off again, this time to South America.*

I wrote to my aunt, 'I'm sitting on my bed in a cheap hotel in Salvador, very well, very happy, completely at peace with this lovely world and living life entirely for the present.'

It was wonderful. There were times when I was sick, wet and cold, out of money, miserable even. I seldom knew during the day where I would sleep that night but I felt I truly came alive when I started to travel. I was directing my own life. It was a marvellous feeling of peace and power that grew the longer I travelled alone.

Sue and I began our South American journey in Brazil. I'd met Sue at a party at my flat in Christchurch in 1972; she'd travelled overland from England across Asia, spent a year or two in Australia and New Zealand, and was intending to return to the UK through the Americas. She was looking for a travelling companion and I jumped at the opportunity. We took a ship to Rio via the Straits of Magellan, and planned to travel north through South America to the USA.

Sue had the trip well organised. While we were together, most of the time we did what she wanted. We slept in hammocks, travelling third class on a boat up the Amazon to Manaus; we hitched out of the jungle town on a Brazilian military plane and we lived in luxury on an estancia in Argentina with friends of Sue's. We slept rough in packing sheds and barns from Terra Del Fuego to Sao Paulo;

dormitory style in cheap hotels with bed bugs, cockroaches and mice. We shivered in the backs of trucks across the freezing Altiplano in Bolivia; squashed up with chickens, produce and packages in local trains and we had our share of frights with border guards who were armed with truncheons and guns.

But by the time we reached Lima, Sue was losing her joy for it all. She'd been travelling for three years and her sights were set on home. She decided she wanted to travel north without delay, whereas I was still fresh. I was excited by the unfamiliar culture, customs, history, places and people. And I loved the simple lifestyle, living one day at a time.

So we parted. I remember standing at the Lima bus station watching the bus pull away and feeling mild panic, wondering, 'What have I done?'. I took in the bustle and the people, the Indians in their bright colours and unique hats, the smart Europeans, the small boys with cheeky smiles, the noise and chatter of a different language – a kaleidoscope of experience. In my mind's eye, I saw the road from Lima, stretching north for miles. I felt very alone, small and insignificant. Yet that day, my life changed.

Up until that point, to a large extent, it was Sue's trip; I had travelled with her as a companion. Now it was all up to me. There was no one else to organise tickets; no one for support when dealing with customs officers; no one to help change money on the black market; no one to consult with at all. After Lima I was completely independent and it gave me an intoxicating sense of freedom I'd never known before.

Although I was alone, I met more people immediately. The route north from Lima was well worn. There were numerous travellers, a large proportion of them North Americans. Most of us 'gringos' were obviously different from the locals. We gathered together at well-established points along the way to trade stories, books, tips and company. We stopped at places of historical and cultural interest like Machu Picchu, or went to 'rest stops' where marijuana, cocaine and mushrooms were part of the culture.

In Ecuador I met a Chilean named Jorge. He was a bit younger than me, about 20 and gorgeous, dark with a brilliant smile and a contagious sense of humour. He was fun to be with, his English was good and I could speak some Spanish. An American friend we spent time with in Quito continually lamented how he'd love to meet Jorge's female equivalent.

Jorge was different from other travellers. He told me he was from a wealthy family. His father had owned several factories in Chile that had been nationalised by the Allende government and they had been thrown out and left with nothing. He was hoping to get to Spain to start afresh.

Jorge was very resourceful. Although he didn't have any money he carried leather to make into belts and purses to sell in the town plazas en route. He had a dream of catching a boat to Spain from

*Libby with local children in Lima.*

Northern Colombia, but it was a long, slow journey, dollar by dollar. He was sometimes frustrated and discouraged, eager to leave South America behind.

A group of us arranged to meet in Popayan in Southern Colombia. Here was another cheap hotel catering to the tastes of foreign travellers (this time scrambled eggs served with hallucinogenic mushrooms).

I planned a long all-day walk with some of the other travellers. Jorge had absolutely no interest in walking and preferred to stay at the hotel to work on his leather wares. He needed to earn money for his escape.

I usually carried all my money, about $US300 in cash, in a money belt strapped round my waist. That day I did something I had never done before; our room could be locked, so I left my money belt under my pillow. Some time before nightfall, I returned to the room to find Jorge had left.

Surprised and feeling suddenly suspicious, I went to my pillow and was relieved to find my money belt, complete with passport and

Sleeping on hammocks on an Amazon river boat.

money, where I had left it. I went out to the courtyard to find someone to talk with.

'Jorge's gone! Did anyone see him?'

There was a general feeling of shock. No one had seen him leave, nor had he said goodbye.

'Is all your stuff intact?' Others were also suspicious.

'Yes. Everything seems to be here.'

'Well, I guess he was just ready to leave and he left.'

'Guess so,' and we left it at that, feeling slightly let down.

Later, after we had eaten, I took out my belt to pay for my food. This time I instinctively knew that some money was missing. I counted and recounted, puzzling it over and decided that I was $30 short. After my initial feeling of disbelief and a brief moment of anger, I began to feel grateful. He'd taken $30, just enough for the bus fare to Cartegena and his boat. Too proud to ask, yet unable to risk the temptation, he had taken only what he needed, no more, no less, to find his freedom.

And now I was alone again.

# DRESSING UP IN MASHHAD

*Ali and Terry Goodall managed to work their passage to the UK in a rather unusual way – Terry as a seaman on a 9000-tonne seagoing fridge called the* PORT BURNIE *out of Gisborne, and Ali as a cabaret singer and entertainer on the cruise liner* NORTHERN STAR. *This was an entertainment in itself, as Ali had never sung cabaret before accepting the job.*

*The couple arranged to join Terry's mother, Rosemary, in Chester. In 1972, after two years at various jobs, they bought a Ford Escort van, put Terry's mother in the back and drove overland to India. They booked a ferry from Madras to Singapore, then flew to Wellington. Ali tells the story.*

If you ever want to smuggle anything, take your mother. Terry's mum was an expert at defusing tense situations. Her warm smile and homely manner soothed sensitive officials ('I've always wanted to come to Bulgaria'), diverted suspicious customs from our cache of black-market rupees ('Would you like a cup of Milo, dear?'), charmed police officials in a dozen countries ('What lovely uniforms') and convinced the religious police that we (young and unmarried) had a reliable chaperone.

This was essential as, by the early 1970s, the overland route was beginning to close. Much of the Muslim world seemed to be in upheaval: Iraq and Syria were closed to travellers, Iran was still ruled by the Shah but seething, there was an acknowledged resentment of 'Western hippies', and tales of attacks on infidel men and women were beginning to filter back to the UK.

So we viewed Iran with a degree of suspicion bordering on

paranoia. Our van had been stoned in Turkey, and one party of Australians travelling in the same direction told us they had barely escaped with their lives; they were travelling by Land Rover, and we kept meeting them in campsites along the way, leapfrogging between Tabriz and Tehran. They had diverted to the ancient city of Qum while we moved on to Isfahan.

Qum was a holy city; the home of the Ayatollah Khomeini. It was the middle of Ramadan, the holy month of fasting and prayer, and unfortunately the two Australian girls were not 'fully covered'. They were jostled and threatened, and had to be rescued by the military police. It was a frightening reminder of the need to be sensitive to religious requirements. We weren't at all keen on putting ourselves in a similar position.

Nevertheless, providing one took care not to offend the dress code, people were incredibly friendly. At every stop we were approached by smiling, laughing students who wanted to practise their English, swap news, discuss politics, and catch up on the fate of Manchester United. (We didn't know as we were Liverpool supporters.)

At one café in Isfahan we met Max and his girlfriend Beljet. We spent some time with them. Max was a very serious student with a slight stutter, well turned out in a dark jacket and white shirt. Beljet was sophisticated and beautiful, with glossy black hair and wonderful brown eyes.

During one conversation, Terry mentioned that we wanted to buy some lapis lazuli or turquoise. Max became animated. Quite the finest turquoise was to be found in Mashhad, and nowhere was there a more hospitable and friendly place than Mashhad. We must certainly visit his cousin, Mohamet, who would help us make a good purchase of turquoise. 'He trades carpets in Mashhad and he will make sure you get the best deals.' At which Max wrote us a note in the most elegant of Parsi script, along with copious instructions on how to get to Mashhad and find his cousin.

Mashhad, north of the great salt desert, was on our route. But after some discussion we decided not to follow Max's advice. The city was known as a religious centre, home of the whirling dervishes and reputed to be a hotbed of religious fervour and intolerance.

مردم ایران دنشان من هستند و من و بلجیت, خیلی مهربانی زرند .

آ نا مسخوا هند در ایران هند عددشت ترکیز بخزد .

خواست كنيم كه به آ نا كمك كنيد وقت مناسب آنا ببينا رکنيد من خيلى مايلم

كه بزودى از نيجه اين ملاقات اطلاع پيدا نم        با تكثر

نارا خدای نگردار نگاهدارم

Max's note.

Terry's paranoia convinced him the note gave specific secret instructions in Parsi to slit our throats and share the spoils. But just outside the city, there was an information booth. We stopped to ask where the nearest campsite was and found that the man inside spoke perfect English.

'Would you mind translating this?' Terry asked, passing over Max's note. Our translator read out: 'These people are my friends and they have been very kind to me and Beljet. They wish to buy some turquoise, so please look after them and get them a good price. I look forward to hearing about the visit soon, your loving cousin Max.'

The tourist official's brilliant and impeccable English was most reassuring: 'You need to make your way towards the centre. When you get to the square next to the holy shrine, you'll need to ask for directions, but there is no problem.' Again, there was an expansive gesture and a broad smile.

*'Mashhad literally means the place of Martyrdom. It is extremely sacred to Shi'ites as the place where the eighth grandson of the prophet Mohammed died in 817. The story spread that the Emām Rezā had been poisoned, so his tomb become a major Shi'ite pilgrimage.'* (Paul Greenway, *Lonely Planet Iran*, 1998).

Most of the city was rather drab: blocks of flats, low houses, small factories and markets. But in the centre, there was the stunning Holy Shrine.

The Āstān-é Ghods-é Razavi was a complex of buildings: the Shah Thamāsbs Minaret, six theological colleges, a golden fountain, two mosques, three museums, 12 halls, two coated entirely with gold, two main and two lesser courtyards, several libraries, barracks and numerous other buildings and halls.

With Terry's worries assuaged, we made our way to the camp on the outskirts of the city. Mum and I changed into a modest dress of long, baggy skirts and loose, long-sleeved tops. We left the van and made our way through the markets towards the city centre. There were hordes of people, some selling live chickens and fruit, some bargaining for goods, as well as musicians and drums. The sights, smells and sounds all combined to create an exotic and exciting atmosphere for this intense religious festival.

It was mid-afternoon by the time we reached the centre. The square was full – with at least 10,000 people: women in full chadors, fierce-looking moustachioed men in dark jackets, berobed mullahs and religious police carrying sticks and guns. The place hummed and throbbed with prayer and fervour.

*Rosemary and Ali in their chadors.*

We were wondering how we would ever find Mohamet's shop in this crowded square, when there was a voice from behind: 'Excuse me, please could you tell me the meaning of your NZ badge?'

Surprised, we turned to confront a handsome young man standing in the doorway of a small shop. After we had explained the meaning of 'NZ' and the fern, we asked if he could please help us find the address of Max's cousin. We passed Max's letter to him.

With a look of astonishment he exclaimed, 'My name is Valli and this is my friend Mohamet, and he is Max's cousin and this is his address!' Quite by chance we had met the people we had set out to find – or rather they had found us in a city square thronging with strangers.

For the next three days, we enjoyed the most wonderful hospitality. Mohamet and Valli enthusiastically entertained and guided us, bargained for our turquoise, demonstrated their carpets, and introduced us to the sights of this holy city.

They took us to see the ceremony of Zurkaneh, a blend of mysticism, powerful rhythm, physical strength and co-ordination to a background throb from drum and gourd and a plaintive male vocal line. Thrilling!

On our last day, Mahomet and Valli arranged between them that we could enter the haram-é motahhar or sacred precinct. This was the great enclosure that surrounds the tomb of the Emām Rezā and we had thought this central area was completely out of bounds to the infidel. We had been careful to stay clear.

But Valli reassured us that only the area immediately around the tomb was forbidden to the unbeliever. Providing we dressed conservatively, and were respectful, there was no prohibition on foreigners in the complex itself. That didn't seem to be too difficult; after all, we would expect visitors to cathedrals in New Zealand to behave with respect.

We nervously followed Valli across the central square to an outer gate. There was an exchange with the gatekeepers, who ducked inside the gate and returned carrying two lengths of black cloth. Mum and I would have to dress in full-length chadors.

This was all very well, but we'd never worn a chador and we

didn't have the first clue how to put it on. The more we tried to manage the slippy, slidy, satiny cloth, the more of a mess we made. Mum started to get the giggles.

Perhaps the rituals of donning and wearing these incredibly awkward and unflattering full veils was a comedy. But there are times and places when it is not wise to laugh. This was a site of huge importance to Islam and as Mum's giggling fits grew worse, Valli began to look concerned, frowning, and muttering, 'This is not good. Not good, not good.'

Just as we were beginning to think it wise to abandon the expedition before the religious police took offence, two fully chadored women appeared with two little girls of about 12 years. The women bent and whispered to the girls, and without saying anything to us, but obviously suppressing their mirth at the incompetence of infidel women, began to arrange and pin our chadors in the acceptable fashion.

When we were fully covered, and had recovered, Valli, in a solemn manner, escorted us into the sacred precinct, where there was a paved courtyard surrounded by an intricately tiled wall. The entrance to the tomb itself (off-limits to foreigners) was a spectacular Persian arch surrounded by Quranic calligraphy. We could see a gilded cupola and single minaret inside. There were museums, containing wonderful artefacts, collections of Islamic ornaments and writing implements, displays of carpets and calligraphy and gifts donated by wealthy pilgrims. There were also cases displaying religious relics.

The two little girls followed us round the entire way and kept us in order. The experience was beautiful, moving and inspiring. We left Mashhad, awed and impressed, but also relieved to be on our way towards the Afghanistan border.

# DUTY BOUND

*Adrienne Coleman was born and raised in Dunedin. She taught for a year at Awahou, a two-teacher school near Wanganui, before flying out in 1974 to join her boyfriend John in London.*

Back in the 1970s, cars in New Zealand were incredibly expensive and not very sophisticated. There were huge duties to protect the New Zealand assembly industry. You could buy Hillmans and old-model Japanese cars, but modern European designs were rare and very pricey.

Duties were high all over the world, but New Zealanders could save substantial sums with a well-established trick. If you were going to Britain on the big OE, you bought a new luxury car on the Continent at the beginning of the trip, thus avoiding British vehicle taxes; and drove it back to Britain, thus avoiding Continental taxes. You could drive the vehicle round Britain for 18 months and then export it back to New Zealand. Back in New Zealand, if you had owned the vehicle for more than one year overseas you didn't have to pay import duty.

If you got the timing right and you managed to keep all the documentation, you could import a luxury vehicle into New Zealand for less than the cost of the much maligned Hillman Hunter. It was a very attractive proposition. It was rumoured you could make enough to pay for the airfare from Britain to New Zealand by importing the right vehicle. Peugeot, Renault and Mercedes were popular, but people brought in all sorts of makes and models.

John was an electronics technician. He had trained with the air force and has always been appreciative of good quality and sound engineering. The idea of owning an up-to-date, sophisticated, late-model Continental car rather appealed to him.

So after he had checked out all the rules and got the appropriate documents, he bought a Peugeot 504 and brought it back to Britain. We were so proud of it. Even now, most people have to put up with old bangers until they are well established. To own a new car in your early twenties, and a luxury model at that, was quite an achievement.

The downside of the system was that you could only stay in Britain for 18 months; then you had to depart, or pay British duty on the car. We planned to leave Britain on the very last of our allotted days, take a Continental tour, then ship the Peugeot back to New Zealand from Rotterdam. It didn't seem very long before our time was up and we were setting off to catch the hovercraft from Dover.

John wanted to have a good look at the hovercraft, as it was very new and exciting. We arrived in Dover in plenty of time and parked on the hard. You could hear the hovercraft coming. It made a fantastic noise and slid out of the water and up the ramp like a space ship in a science fiction movie.

We jumped out of the car to take a photograph, covering our ears to keep out the noise. When we turned back to the car, we found we had slammed the doors shut and the keys were still in the ignition. Sophisticated car it might be, but even the French hadn't worked out how to stop people locking their keys inside.

Absolute panic stations. This was the last journey out that the hovercraft was going to make that day. If we didn't get on the hovercraft, we would have to stay in Britain. If we had to stay in Britain we would have to pay duty. Lots of duty.

John went to the ticket office to ask if they could help, but no, they couldn't. We asked other passengers if they could help – no they couldn't. The nearest garage was several miles away. And while we pulled and rattled the door locks, trucks and cars were driving down the ramp and disappearing inside the hovercraft. We stood at the top of the loading ramp feeling increasingly desperate.

John went down into the hovercraft to talk to the crew.

It's in times like these when you discover how incredibly nice people can be. The engineer from the hovercraft came off the boat in his uniform, carrying a piece of wire. He bent the end of the wire into a U with a pair of pliers, pushed the bend down through the door seal and wiggled the end of the wire until it caught the door lock. We watched with bated breath. Slowly, slowly, he pulled the wire. It slipped off. More tension, more wiggling. This time it caught: the wire began to straighten and the knob popped free. We breathed a huge sigh of relief, pulled open the doors, turned on the ignition and drove down the ramp to squeeze into the very last place on the vehicle deck.

We had our Continental tour and flew back via Los Angeles. The Peugeot was shipped back to New Zealand from Holland. It was a lovely car. We kept it until 1986.

# FIREFLIES ON THE ADRIATIC

Allan and Ruth Polson are both conscious of their Scottish ancestry. They grew up listening to the laments from their grandparents. The stories of the Highland clearances have been passed from generation to generation, growing at each telling.

So the first part of their trip was to visit the places their grandfathers had come from. In Helmsdale and Banff, Port Patrick and Sutherland, they felt they were breathing the air, eating the food and walking the streets with their ancestors' ghosts.

The second purpose of the journey was to see Europe. 'We hadn't travelled when we were younger, and we wanted to see a bit of the world while the children were young enough to do things with.' Travelling with young children is different — the time table, the pace and agenda must all suit the demands and needs of the younger members of the party.

Ruth tells their story.

The Polson children on the beach at Dubrovnik.

At the time, Allan was a health inspector, and I was into motherhood between spells as a teacher. Allan arranged four months' leave and, in 1976, we flew to England via Singapore and Hong Kong.

It was just as well the children were small, since the Commer van we'd hired was not large. It was about the size of two queen-size beds, with a tiny stove and fridge, two bunks at the top, and two below.

David, who was nine, slept across the front, Rachael, aged seven, took the top bunk, while Allan and I slept in the back with Matthew who was two. It is actually easier travelling with children by campervan, rather than by organised tour, because it allows you to be flexible. If it was too hot, for example, we could go to bed late, and get up later. We had a settled routine of food gathering and trip planning; leaving the campgrounds about 10 am to grind our slow 100 kilometres of frequent stops and small excursions to spend the afternoon somewhere of interest: at a beach or museum, art gallery or cathedral, or simply to wander through medieval streets,

Small children open doors. Ours were very blonde and blue eyed, and stood out especially in Mediterranean countries. They were always being patted and loved and needing rescue from old ladies pinching their cheeks and gushing baby talk in a dozen different languages. If we ever got lost, or needed someone to go the extra mile, then the sight of a blonde head poking out the door was a passport to goodwill.

A child's view of travel is very different from that of an adult. Twenty years later, they remember Van Goghs, swimming in the Mediterranean, electrical storms and snakes in the grass. They have forgotten the place names, motorway hassles and the tedium of travelling.

We took a few small toys. Every time we stopped for petrol Matthew would climb out the van, grab a handful of pebbles or earth, and bring it back to put in his digger trucks. By the time we completed the tour the back of the van rattled with gravel spilt into the cracks and crevices.

And children have no trouble with language – they could play with anyone. The camping grounds were their world; did it matter if it was in Rome or London?

The most important task was to keep everyone fed and watered. Breakfast would always be cereal and fruit of one sort or another. We bought local food where possible, and that meant plenty of rice and fruit. We ate few potatoes and little meat, as these go off in the heat. Instead, there were different varieties of bread and cheese in almost every village. We feasted on pizzas in Italy, baguettes in France, apple strudel in Austria and if we were still hungry late at night, Allan would cook pancakes on our tiny stove to eat with lemon juice and sugar.

We were travelling north through Yugoslavia, somewhere north of Dubrovnik, when we decided to drop off the main highway and camp on the coast. We came to one of those little Adriatic villages; it was like stepping back 200 years.

Long, low houses with stone tiles black with smoke and tar. Carts of produce were hauled by depressed-looking donkeys, old women dressed in black sitting on stools spinning with old-fashioned spindles.

Down on the beach was a tavern set amongst small trees and stone walls. Allan pulled the van into the car park. Behind the building, there was a large spit roasting a whole sheep, turned by two older men wearing drab jackets and flat caps. The turning meat spitting into the coals sent the most delicious smell drifting along the beach.

We sat drinking cheap red Yugoslav wine as the sun set very slowly over the Adriatic Sea. The children were playing on the beach as the light changed through yellow to orange, red and blue, and all the while, the two spit roasters slowly turned the handle over glowing coals with low murmuring and laughter in another language.

When the light had faded, the people of the taverna carved great chunks from the roast onto plates with a thick slab of bread and spring onion and dipped in crystalline salt. Delicious and succulent; no other vegetables – not like the New Zealand meat and two veg in watery gravy followed by pudding and coffee. It was just a perfect sunset and happy children playing on the beach to the soft sound of waves.

And later, in the pitch dark, there were fireflies dancing in the starlight. 'Look, fairy lights' we said to the children. 'Hush or they'll go out.' Better than fireworks, better than Disneyland. Real magic.

*Waiting for lamb to cook on the spit.*

# ELEPHANTS TRIP ON GUY ROPES

*For Gillian Oppenheim, travel was the under-26 thing. She took the
AUSTRALIS from Auckland to Sydney, and then on to Melbourne,
Fiji, the Panama Canal and Europe.*

*She took her first job in France with the Vicomtesse Jacqueline de
Prémont, a former European champion horsewoman. The stables
were unbelievable; horses were treated like royalty and shared their
lodging with the biggest rats in France. There was a beautiful
chateau inhabited by an ageing butler and his two sisters, but there
was only one tap and no electricity. It was all a bit lonely, so after
three months, Gillian headed to England for a round of the 'usual
pub and teaching jobs. Opportunities are huge if you grab them:
Billingsgate fish market at four in the morning, Ascot, the Royal
Garden Party and amazing live-in jobs in manors and pubs all over
Britain and Ireland.' In 1972, Gillian set off home via Africa.*

The African overland safari was run by Kimbla Travel Ltd. The
brochure opens: 'If you're young (under 30) and looking for a trip of
a lifetime, a trip with a thrill of adventure and the anticipation of
the unexpected around every corner, join Kimbla's Camping Safari
and explore with us East, Central and Southern Africa.' I'm not sure
that the over-thirty-year-olds would agree on the definition of
young, but the advertising was accurate in one aspect – a deluxe
tour it was not.

We started off in two long-wheel-base Land Rovers towing trailers.
The tour started in Nairobi and the plan was to travel through the
game parks into Uganda, down through Zaire, Tanzania, Malawi,
Zambia, Zimbabwe (then Rhodesia) and finish in South Africa.

Most nights we'd build a campfire and sleep around it. There were all these wonderful noises – little coughs and splutters, high cries and then the eyes of foxes and bandicoots shining in the dark. During the day, we'd see beautiful butterflies, the occasional antelope, boys and men herding cattle and goats, and women carrying huge loads on their heads. Everything went on their heads, from bundles of clothes to cans of kerosene, as they swayed along with straight backs and elegant strides. The land was so brown. All the colour was in the people with their bright, wraparound dresses and their brilliant smiles.

When you are on a trip like that, you don't read papers or listen to the radio; you just travel and enjoy the party. But this was August 1972 and Idi Amin had just come to power in Uganda. We knew something was up, because every time we stopped, Indians would come up to trade currency on the black market. There was an undercurrent of tension and threat, but we ignored the warning signs and travelled on.

Our last stop in Uganda was to be the Murchison Falls National Park. From there we intended to cross into Zaire. At the entrance to Murchison there was a buffalo skull sitting on top of a large sign which read in block capitals:

### CAMPERS

UNDER NO CIRCUMSTANCES
SHOULD WILD ANIMALS BE FED.
ALL FOOD SHOULD BE KEPT
IN THE VEHICLE AT NIGHT
AND NOT IN THE TENT.

TENTS SHOULD NOT BE PITCHED
CLOSE TOGETHER.
SPACE SHOULD BE ALLOWED
FOR ANIMALS TO MOVE
FREELY IN THE CAMP.
UNDER NO CIRCUMSTANCES
SHOULD CAMPERS SLEEP
IN THE OPEN.

Sign at the entrance to
the Murchison Falls
National Park.

We looked at the notice and laughed: 'What's going to happen? Poor little elephants might trip over our guy ropes, ha ha ha.' It didn't seem very likely, but it was raining so we duly put up the tents. We prepared the meal, sat and chatted for a while, then went to bed.

At about midnight, there was this terrible crashing and banging sound. One of our party, Suzie Hatchwell, got up to see what it was. She found four elephants investigating the trailers (which they eventually turned over to get at our mealy maize and food).

Surprised by the sight of the elephants, she turned to run. As she came running back, yelling and screaming, 'There are elephants in the trailer!', she tripped over a guy rope and collapsed in a heap on the ground.

The camp erupted into chaos. Some of us were trying to find cameras, others were gawking at the huge beasts. How do you chase away an elephant? Call shoo?

When the herd had galumphed off into the night and we'd all calmed down, we got to look at poor Suzie. She was sitting on the ground nursing her ankle and looking very uncomfortable. It was quite obviously broken.

Any travel injury is serious, but most minor injuries of this nature are soon patched up in any reasonably equipped hospital or clinic. In this case, the nearest major hospital was in Kampala, about 250 kilometres along dirt roads back the way we'd come. Looking at the map, Peter found a mission in Zaire just the other side of the border. We were sure they would have a clinic where a broken ankle could be set.

But first we had to get there. The border crossing was manned by surly-looking guards, wearing odd bits and pieces of uniform, red-eyed with dak and maize beer, and toting automatic rifles. They were unpleasant, aggressive and frightening, and insisted we weren't allowed to take any foreign currency out of Uganda.

It was obviously a ruse. Peter walked around whispering to each member of the party, 'Don't hand over your money, don't hand it over.' The guards turned the guns on him and for a moment we thought Peter would be assaulted or shot.

About an hour later, we were allowed to cross and we made our way to the Beni Mission. But the mission wasn't able to provide a great deal of help; it turned out to be a leper colony run by nuns. The only medical practitioner was the local witch doctor. Although he wore a white coat, the surgery was a mud hut, full of bottled frogs legs, snake skins and unhealthy-looking potions. What Suzie really needed was an X-ray, plaster of Paris and a comfortable bed for a few nights.

Although the 'doctor' was able to bandage Sue's leg, it was obvious that we had to get to a proper hospital. The nearest town to the south was well over 1000 kilometres away along muddy tracks and river crossings. What is more, Suzie and a couple of others in the party were developing malaria. There was nothing for it but to head back across the border to Kampala. At least it had a well-equipped hospital and some tar-sealed roads.

This time, when we approached the border crossing, we took all our cash and stuffed it behind the headlights of the Land Rover. Just as well, since the border guards did their best to take everything apart. We sat in the sun, depressed and disconsolate as the thugs ripped open the seats and emptied the bottles on the ground. They even pulled the Tampax apart. Sheer vandalism. We spent eight hours lined up on the border. Poor Suzie must have been in dreadful pain but somehow she survived it all.

It took us two more days to get to Kampala, and we spent three more days there before Suzie and the other malarial travellers were fit enough to carry on. By this time we were well aware of the deteriorating situation in Uganda, so we fled to Tanzania as fast as we could.

Compared with Uganda, the rest of the trip went smoothly. We had a wonderful time, but by the stage we got to Johannesburg, I just wanted to get home. I remember going to a store and buying new clothes; after three months on the road, we must have stunk to high heaven. I threw all my old clothes in a rubbish bin and headed straight to the airport, from where I flew out to Australia.

*Elephants in the campsite!*

## LA MAR REINA

*Canals are unfamiliar to many New Zealanders, but a network of waterways criss-cross Europe, connecting all major cities. The first canals were built in the 14th century to ship heavy goods such as stone to build the great cathedrals, and although many canals fell into disuse at the end of the 19th century, it is still possible to 'sail' from London to Brussels up the Rhine, down to Paris, across to the Rhône, and from Bordeaux to Marseilles. On the slow way are some of the greatest engineering and architectural sights in Europe.*

*Isabel Mitchell is a fourth-generation New Zealander who was 'mad keen' on travelling. In 1971, she was invited to spend six months with her friend Judy Murray and her family, Aunt Mil and Uncle John from Rotorua, exploring Europe by canal.*

Uncle John was very well organised, but had no boating experience. Somehow, he had got it into his head that he would like to explore Europe by canal. We left on the *Northern Star* in April 1971 and spent six weeks in London until John found a suitable boat. *La Mar Reina* was a 28-foot launch with a diesel engine. There was not much space on board for two adults and two teenage girls – it only had 14 feet of cabin space.

We spent some time learning how to navigate before motoring down the Thames, and around the coast to Ramsgate, where we waited for a pilot to take us across to Dunkirk. From there we motored slowly through the inland waters of Belgium, Holland, up the Rhine into Germany, then via the Seine to Paris, across to the Rhône and down into the Mediterranean.

It is a most extraordinary way to travel – so much more leisurely than by road or rail. There is the gentle thump-thump of the diesel engine; the passage is slow with a stop every few kilometres to wait for a lock or another boat. There is plenty of time to absorb the marvellous views of the chateaux and churches, of little villages with crowded houses and cafés; old farmhouses with slate or tiled roofs, and pretty lock-keepers' cottages with flower gardens, vineyards, woods and meadows. The colours and houses are just so different from the New Zealand landscape. In remote areas of France, the villagers wore clogs and black shawls and still drew water from wells. It felt like a sort of time travel, back to a slower age, remote from the bustle and haste of modern life.

Each night we'd stop when we got hungry and tie up to a wharf close to a village. We would eat in the boat or sometimes at a local restaurant. You could buy huge German potato pancakes and sip cheap local wine. Most of the wine we bought wasn't very good; there were some very rough red wines in France, which made your mouth pucker up and were probably best diluted with water or lemonade. However, travellers soon get accustomed to rough wines and strange tastes, and you eat and drink what you can afford.

Late one night on the Rhine, John tied up at a small jetty. It was getting dark, it rained and we were tired and anxious to get on with supper and have a rest. There was no one around and we soon had supper on the cabin table: rye bread, tinned English mackerel and cheap, chateau-cardboard wine.

We were just sitting down to eat when there was a tremendous thumping on the cabin roof. John opened the hatch and outside was a big German gentleman, looking and sounding very irate.

'Was tun Sie hier! Können sie das Schild nicht lesen*?' He was pointing to a small sign. We leaned out the hatch and squinted into the gloom at a sign reading 'Kein Anlegeplatz' in Gothic script.

Uncle John was remarkably good at placating angry people. 'I'm terribly sorry,' he said, smiling. 'Didn't see the sign at all, but we are just having a bite of supper. Would you care to join us?' He gestured into the cabin.

---

* 'What do you think you are doing here. Can't you read the sign?'

La Mar Reina *leaving Paris on the Seine, bound for Lyon.*

Before the jetty owner knew what was happening, he had been ushered into the cabin and was squashed into a berth between two teenage girls. Aunt Mil set out another place, and Uncle John poured him a glass of our stock red plonk. We were soon talking in broken English and German and managed to tell him that we were from New Zealand and on holiday by boat. Our guest seemed to be rather enjoying himself, tucking into rye and mackerel with gusto, but taking hesitant sips of wine.

It was a bit of a squash in the small cabin and it was soon beginning to fog up. After we had eaten, the jetty owner stood up and, smacking his hand on the table, asked: 'Sie trinken gern Wein? Kommen Sie, wir wollen ein Glas Wein zusammen trinken*.' Beckoning vigorously, he pointed out to the jetty.

We clambered out of the boat, and just behind the sign was a large, very shiny black Mercedes. We were ushered into deep leather seats in the back and then shot off round the corner and up

---

\* 'You like to drink wine. Come with me we'll have a drink together.'

a track, leaving a spray of gravel. In the dusk we could see lights burning in a group of buildings at the top of the hill. We were taken to a long, low-lying stone building at the side of a large manor house lined with row after row of barrels. We had landed at a vineyard jetty.

Our host then went from barrel to barrel, easing back the bungs and sniffing with intense concentration. When he found a barrel with wine to meet his standards, he carefully siphoned out enough to fill small glasses and passed the wine around. They were magnificent: smooth, fruity, aromatic, wonderful-tasting wines. Barrel after barrel, glass after glass – quite what he had thought of Uncle John's cardboard chateau, I don't know. But I'll remember the taste of those wonderful wines for many years, though we were somewhat the worse for wear when we returned to the boat.

We continued our journey from the Rhine to the Mosel, linked to Metz, then into the Seine and down the Rhône to Marseilles where we sold *La Mar Reina* to an Italian. Judy and I flew back from Monte Carlo to Canada, before returning to New Zealand.

# TWO STROKES AND FOUR

*Dave Robinson left New Zealand in May 1975 with the aim of going to the Motorcycle TT Races in the Isle of Man. He comes from a farming background and soon found work as a relief milker at Aireyholme Farm in Great Ayton where Captain Cook's father had been the manager.*

*Not much seemed to have changed since Captain Cook's day. The farm was mixed meat and dairy, milking 50 cows and running dry stock and sheep on the moors. It was real James Herriot country with long, low stone barns and high dry-stone walls.*

*But public transport also seemed not to have developed greatly since Cook's day! There was no easy way to travel out of the Yorkshire Dales, so Dave bought a Honda four-stroke motorcycle to travel through England and Europe.*

Despite its 125 cc, it was a beaut machine. Never missed a beat all the way round Holland and Germany, up to the Arctic Circle, through Denmark and Norway, down through Czechoslovakia and Austria at a top speed of 80 kilometres an hour. Up and down the gears, tailgating lorries – you can't go to sleep on a motorbike.

I aimed to travel about 200 kilometres a day, which was more or less a tankful of petrol, stopping off whenever I felt like it in remote areas to camp or to tour museums, castles or towns.

Every Sunday, I'd have a rest day on which I'd do my washing, give the bike a once-over, change the oil, tighten the chain and do all the little things that keep a machine going smoothly. Look after a machine and it'll look after you.

I'd met a German guy at a youth hostel near Land's End, who said he'd show me around Berlin. That's if I could get there. The mid-1970s were the height of East-West tension. The wall was still in place and there were lots of stories of escapes and shootings. But I thought I'd go and have a look.

To get to Berlin, you had to drive through the Berlin Corridor, which was an autobahn and rail link from Hamburg through East Germany to West Berlin. It would be a trip of about 200 kilometres and there was a petrol station marked on the map.

At the start of the Corridor you were given all sorts of dire warnings not to leave the motorway: not to stop, or depart from the route. They were as hard as nails, those border guards – they really put the wind up me.

So I started off along the Corridor feeling threatened and worried. After about an hour into the trip, I began to get really worried. The little tank on the bike didn't hold that much petrol and I hadn't seen any sign of the petrol station.

I slowed down to save a bit of petrol, but after another 20 minutes or so I knew I was going to run out of gas. I thought about leaving the motorway and looking for a petrol station in a village, but decided against it. I'd heard about people going missing, and I'd read some Cold War stories, so I wasn't about to test the fiction.

You get really tense when you know something bad is going to happen to you. I kept riding, more and more uptight, turned on to reserve, but eventually the engine began to cough and splutter, and then conked out. I pulled over to the side, took off my jacket and helmet, and looked around for a few minutes.

Nothing for it but to start pushing the bike. I hadn't a clue how far the next petrol station was, or whether or not I would have to push the bike all the way to Berlin; maybe the map was wrong. So I just kept slogging along, one foot after the other. Well, I hadn't been pushing that long, when a little blue Trabant pulled over.

Anyone who travelled in Eastern Europe in the 1970s will remember these vehicles. The body was built out of fibreglass, powered by a shocking 'Ersatz' two-stroke engine, which spewed out smoke and smelt awful. The finish was awful, the ride noisy and uncomfortable, and compared with Western and Japanese engines and cars, the Trabant was back with horses and carts. They're probably collector's items by now.

So out climbed this guy, a bit older than me; jovial sort of look but slightly overweight. He walked up to me and started talking in German. I don't speak German and he didn't speak English, but we managed all the same. I pointed at the petrol tank, and said, 'Finito, kaputt, it's finished, no petrol, all gone.'

He obviously got the idea, as he pointed at his car.

'Ich kann Ihnen etwas Benzin geben.'

I didn't have a clue what he was talking about, but he walked to the back of the Trabant, pulled out a battered can and gave me a thumbs-up. You don't need a translation for that. He gave the can a shake, and I could hear a bit of fuel sloshing around in the bottom. But as this was two stroke and probably not very good two stroke at that, and my 125 cc was a highly tuned four stroke and used to much more refined fuel, I wasn't sure what was going to happen.

Ah well, I thought, it's only a bit of oil after all. So we poured just under a litre of two-stroke fuel into the tank. It didn't quite fill up the tank but I figured that it would get me to Berlin or the next petrol station.

I rummaged in my pocket and found some Western Deutschmarks. There weren't very many of those either, but his face absolutely lit up. It was probably worth 10 times as much to him as it was to me, as East Germans weren't allowed to have West German currency. Then he said, 'Folgen sie mir, bitte! Drei Kilometer von hier ist eine Tankstelle, wo sie tanken können,' and motioned to me to follow him.

I put my helmet and jacket back on, primed the carburettor and after a couple of kicks, the engine fired, revved and we were away.

We'd only driven a couple of kilometres when the Trabant turned off towards a village, the driver waving through the window for me to follow. So I swallowed my fears and followed the smoke trail into a small petrol station. There seemed to be a lot of security guards wandering around, so I thought I'd better not say too much or I might get him into trouble. I gave him a quick wink, a polite smile and mouthed a 'Danke schön'. He grinned and went on his way, leaving me to fill up with the real stuff.

That fill of petrol took me all the way through to Berlin, and I made sure to give the bike an extra-thorough once-over that weekend. I went on from Berlin through Dresden, into Czecho-slovakia and back to Austria.

Getting back to the West was such a relief. The towns and people in Eastern Europe seemed so drab and dreary, the colours depressing and the sky grey. There were troops and men in uniforms everywhere. Apparently there were two million Russians in Czechoslovakia, all of whom had to be fed and housed by the Czechs. The farming wasn't that developed; they were still using horses and carts to get the hay in and do the ploughing. It was very picturesque, but not very efficient.

When you came to the borders, you had to ride through zigzags and huge blocks the size of a small car. There would be three or four stops at each point. The guards were so thorough and so cold; they put the passport up to your face, looked at the photo, then they looked at you again, about three times. Then the next guard would do the same and the one after that too. This went on and on – all to make sure that none of the guards' relatives got out.

There would be a machine gun tower in the paddock out to the right, with rolls of barbed wire around the border and big Alsatian dogs straining on leads. That's when I started to wonder, 'Am I really going to get out of here?' In New Zealand barbed wire is used for farm fences and animals. All this to stop people from getting out?

In Berlin, there was a very emotional crowd of people standing around crying and saying farewell, leaving friends and relatives behind in the East. I had a paper with New Zealand stamped on it, so I could go through the gates and into West Germany where the streets were clean and bright, the people were smiling and you could eat McDonald's and read the papers. And all these people behind me who didn't have this paper couldn't get through and couldn't say what they thought or felt.

And then there were the guys like the one in the Trabant, who stop and pull over and help when they see that you are in trouble. And that is what I remember: not the borders and the hassles and threats or even the castles, waterfalls and museums. It's the people. People all around the world have pretty much the same aspirations, but places like East Germany and Berlin really made me appreciate New Zealand.

## MOST USEFUL ITEM

Jackie Napier considers that the most useful item to have in the desert is an umbrella.

Wherever you are, sooner or later you have to go to the loo. And you can guarantee that just as soon as you are getting comfortable, there will be a grind of gears, and over the rise will come another vehicle, usually a bus packed full of gawking passengers. A raised umbrella guarantees privacy in at least one direction.

# UP AGAINST THE WALL IN RIO CUARTO

*Shona Thompson is a third-generation New Zealander, originally
from Takapau. She left New Zealand in 1973 to study for an MA at
the University of Alberta in Canada. In 1975 she was joined by her
friend Lyn and the two booked a trip through South America with a
London-based company called Encounter Overland.*

There were 22 of us at the start, but by the time we reached the end
of our trip in Buenos Aires five months later, seven had dropped out.
It was a pretty rough trip, travelling on the back of an old, ex-British
Army Bedford truck with canopy sides that were mostly left rolled
up. It was only the second trip Encounter Overland had done
through South America and neither the New Zealand driver, Ken,
nor his co-pilot Johno had done this run before. We found ourselves
on some very hairy roads at times.

We joined the truck in Cartegena in Colombia, then travelled
down through Ecuador, Peru, into Bolivia, Paraguay and Argentina.
On board were four New Zealanders, a couple of Australians, six
Swiss, four Brits and others from the USA and Germany. Although
it was rough, dusty and uncomfortable it was also very exciting and
lots of fun. Most of the time we camped on the side of the road,
sleeping under the stars or around a fire, huddled in ponchos and
blankets. We towed a trailer that carried the tents we used when it
was wet or very cold.

There was little storage on the truck, so every day we would have
to find a local market where the rostered cooks could shop for the
next three meals. Sometimes it was quite difficult to find food, but
it got noticeably better as soon as we crossed into Argentina. Here

*The Encounter Overland truck on a mountain pass in Peru.*

we could buy fresh vegetables and huge steaks – and very cheaply at that. After several weeks of sparse food in the high altiplano of Peru and Bolivia, good meat and vegetables were a treat. So was the abundance of good red wine, which was very cheap too.

You don't generally read papers while you're travelling and I don't think any of us were really aware of what was happening in Argentina at the time. But looking back, this was at the height of el guerra sucia, the dirty war. Despite the sophistication of the cities and the apparent tranquillity of the countryside, there was an incipient revolution going on.

Early one morning we stopped in a town called Rio Cuarto, south of Cordoba. While the rostered cooks went off to shop as usual, the remainder of the party explored the town. After four months of travel we were scruffy and unkempt; I expect we could have all done with a good wash. When we arrived in these small towns in our big, bright-orange truck we usually drew a fair bit of attention anyway.

This particular day we got back to the truck at the agreed time and found a very nervous-looking Ken surrounded by armed police. He kept saying, 'Get into the truck, just don't argue, just get into the truck!' We couldn't figure out what was going on, but Ken was very jumpy so we got in. From there we could see that there was a policeman in the cab with Ken, his gun pointed Ken's way.

The truck followed a police vehicle around the corner and stopped outside the police station. We were immediately surrounded by armed guards who yelled at us to get out, pointing guns and sounding mean. So out we tumbled and were marched single file into the police station courtyard and faced against the wall, hands up and spread out like a scene from a movie.

By this stage we all realised that this was fairly drastic. John, one of the other New Zealanders, turned around to see what was going on and got a rifle butt slammed into his back. He told us afterwards that at that moment he experienced what it was like to be 'scared shitless'. Fortunately, I was up against a window. It had been painted over light green, the same colour as the walls, and in it I could see the reflections of the policemen behind us. Most of them were young, probably younger than us, and I could tell by the way they were goofing around and laughing that they weren't really intent on shooting us.

A party of police went to search the truck, turfing out travel-stained backpacks and well-used ponchos. It must have soon become obvious that these 15 rather scruffy individuals were unlikely revolutionaries. There were no bombs, no guns, no ammunition. Instead they found a cache of international passports and lots of cheap trinket souvenirs. Obviously touristos!

Now what? Here were all these young men in their important uniforms, full of bravado and toting submachine guns, who didn't know what to do with their captives. And here was a group of tourists, now getting a little stroppy and wanting to go and have lunch.

Barbara, one of the Swiss girls, spoke fluent Spanish, so she and Ken began negotiating with the police. On and on the police went, pointing to our passports, with lots of expression and arm waving. Apparently the one officer who could authorise our release was out of town and not due back until much later in the day.

When in doubt, officialdom fills in forms. Apart from anything else it passes the time and makes one feel important.

We were to be interviewed, but as none of the police spoke English or German the first couple of interviews were painfully slow. We couldn't understand them and they couldn't understand us. So Barbara ended up as the police interpreter. She soon learned how to speed things up and with each new interview the interrogations became more and more farcical.

One by one we'd be formally ushered into a small, bleak room. By the time it was my turn, I walked in to find Barbara sitting behind a huge desk at an old typewriter. Beside her stood the police lieutenant, with his chest puffed out and trying to look important. The interrogation went like this:

The officer would bark, 'Nombre?'

And Barbara would say 'Name', and start typing it before the answer came out.

Then the interrogator would again bark, 'Hermano y hermana?'.

And Barbara would say, 'How many brothers and sisters just say one', making it simple for herself because she knew she would then be asked to record all their names and ages.

Then the officer would say, 'De dónde es?', and Barbara would say, 'Where were you born make it simple', anticipating having to type a word like, in my case, Waipukurau.

And on it went. Finally, after eight hours, they let us go. We piled back into the truck and drove out of town as fast as we could. It was dark by then and we had trouble finding a campsite.

That night we spent a long time sitting around a campfire mulling over the day and sharing our thoughts. Barbara was our hero, but other responses were interesting. The Aussies and Kiwis among us had never really felt as though we were in any great danger. After the initial shock it was mostly an adventure. Yeah, soldiers and guns are pretty nasty, but travellers don't get shot, now do they?

The Europeans, on the other hand, had been very worried. I guess, having learnt from their history, they know that innocent people do get shot and killed. Some had seriously thought they would be.

Although Argentina was much more developed than the other South American countries, we became increasingly aware of the tensions and dangers. In Buenos Aires we regularly heard gunshots at night, and we'd often turn corners to find whole streets cordoned off and armed soldiers running everywhere. It felt like a dicey place to be, despite its sophistication, and we were quite relieved to move on.

# CANE GARDEN BAY

Shona Thompson and her friend Lyn arrived on the island of Tortola in the British Virgin Islands, equipped with a fishing rod and a small tent, in January 1976. After several months of a Canadian prairie winter they had decided that the balmy Caribbean was the place to be.

The campsite on Tortola.

Tortola was just a short ferry trip from Charlotte Amalie in the US Virgin Islands, but not nearly as developed or frenetic with tourists. Nor was there a camping ground. After spending our first night camping, unwisely, under a coconut tree beside the Chase Manhattan Bank in Road Town, the locals suggested we go over the hill to the beach on the other side of the island. So off we went and found the most beautiful place – Cane Garden Bay. Wonderful white sand, little waves lapping on the shore and palm trees, just picture perfect. We went to one end of the bay, found a level spot in the vegetation beyond the sand, pitched our little tent and stayed there for weeks.

During the day we lay on the sand and soaked up the sun, working through our heat deficit from the Canadian winter, letting the quiet and peacefulness soak into our souls. We watched the odd sailboat come and go, and the pelicans diving.

At night we could lie in the tent and listen to the sounds of the waves, the screech and hum of strange birds and insects, and the wonderful exotic rhythms of a steel band issuing from Stanley's Welcome Bar.

Stanley's Welcome Bar was the grand name for a blue concrete structure, mostly pillars, supporting a tin roof and open on three sides. It was right on the beach in the middle of the bay, and it was where both the locals and the yachties drank. Stanley was a tall, thin, leathery black man of about 40, seemingly old to us youngsters in our twenties. He was very genial and laid back, and didn't mind us using his toilet or tap water. Most of the day he spent sitting behind a telescope looking out across the water.

We had very little money so we lived on coconuts collected from the beach. An older man named Isaac, older than Stanley, would open them for us with his machete. It sounds romantic, but a diet of coconuts can give you dreadful diarrhoea and the insects could be fearsome at night. We were soon covered with ferocious bites.

Occasionally, we'd hitch or take the little local bus to Road Town to check for mail at Poste Restante and buy coconut buns. Coconut buns were a local speciality, really big and really cheap. They lasted for days. We tried fishing off the jetty, dangling a line baited with

*Stanley's Welcome Bar.*

cheese above little, brightly coloured tropical fish. I don't think the fish were ever in any danger.

In retrospect, it was a bizarre and naïve thing to do; to arrive on a tropical resort island, pitch a tent and expect to live there. But that is what we did and no one seemed to mind. Eventually, with dwindling finances, we resorted to taking jobs as cooks on charter yachts. This meant a roof over our heads, decent food (if we cooked it) and the chance to explore the other islands. We were paid something like $US10 a day while on charter. In all, we spent about two months in the Virgin Islands.

Ten years later we went back to Cane Garden Bay. By this time Lyn had a husband and a three-month-old baby, and they owned a yacht on which they had sailed from the UK.

My partner and I, on holiday from our now respectable jobs in New Zealand, met them in Barbados and we set sail for our idyll. Having spent so many hours, years earlier, gazing from our squalid campsite at sailboats moored peacefully in the bay, it was a strangely emotional experience to be returning there on our own beautiful boat. But they were very mixed emotions.

The bay was full of sailboats. Stanley's Welcome Bar was still there, looking much the same. So was Stanley. He admitted to recognising us only after we pointed out the New Zealand $1 note pinned on the wall behind his bar, which we'd given him. The old rubber tyre still hung from a palm tree out the front and the pelicans were still diving. But a hotel and bar had been built on our favourite part of the beach, big, bright and brash. They hired out paddleboats, hoby cats and jet skis, and these were all crowded on the sand around the little, curved palm tree that we had loved the most.

We sailed away. Who knows what it's like there now.

# TWO-MINUTE NOODLES

*Since 1977, Didi Muncaster-Wright has travelled regularly through Asia and the Pacific. She has worked in the Solomon Islands, and travelled in Thailand, Laos, Malaysia, Singapore and Cambodia. In 1996, she and Simon Hayman took a barge up the Mekong River from Louangphrabang to Yuxi Shi.*

The only transport up-river was an ancient, rusting vessel about 60 feet long, powered by an unreliable diesel engine. The journey was supposed to take three days and the 'captain' assured us that the fare of $6 included accommodation and evening meals.

What a bargain, we thought. We returned into the village to buy a few rice cakes and cans of soft drink, then joined the rest of the passengers on deck. We were told to be at the jetty by 8.30 am or we would miss the boat.

It wasn't until 11.30 am that the engines started. The barge was overloaded with about 200 passengers, their livestock, small babies, grandparents, goods and parcels for delivery upstream. The passengers played games, gambled and talked while the barge thud-thudded slowly upstream through jungle punctuated by small clearings and paddy fields.

Each night, we would stop at a small village. The houses, built of palm and bamboo, stood on stilts above the flood plain; the walls were open to the air and mosquitoes. Livestock, pigs and chickens were tied underneath.

Most of the passengers would disembark and disappear to stay with relatives or friends. We were escorted to the village guesthouse, which was no more sophisticated than the rest of the village.

We were introduced to the hostess, who, after much mutually incomprehensible conversation, would begin preparing the evening meal over an open fire. It was strictly one-pot cooking.

We had been looking forward to sampling the local cuisine. I've always been interested in differing tastes and experiences. These days you can taste fine Thai and Vietnamese cooking in well equipped restaurants and bars in almost every major New Zealand town, in 1977, Eastern cooking was less familiar.

What's more, the ordinary village people of these countries do not eat nearly as well as we might imagine when we look at the 101 menu items available in our ethnic restaurants: most of the villagers ate unflavoured rice or noodles. There was no additional meat or fish, or stir-fried vegetables with exotic spices to provide variety and balance.

Nevertheless, we paying foreigners were to be treated differently. Local food was not good enough – only the best would do. On our first night we watched the hostess light a fire, anticipating a mouthwatering genuine local cuisine. She boiled water and took a packet of noodles from an open cupboard: not the locally made noodles, but a specially imported foreign brand. I recognised a familiar-looking, yellow packet, Maggi Two Minute Noodles, beef flavour, made in New Zealand.

# AND THE BEAT GOES ON

*Most of the stories in this book are about travel in the 1960s and 70s, but New Zealanders still travel all over the world. There is magic in travel for travel's sake.*

*Sarah McCarter flew to the UK early in 2000 and then travelled by train and bus through Holland, France, Germany, the Czech Republic and Austria. She arrived in Salzburg late in November.*

Wherever you travel, you keep meeting people on the same backpackers' trail – Americans, Canadians, Australians, South Americans and New Zealanders. 'See you in Berlin for the demo'; 'Go to Uncle Toby's in Prague'; 'I'll be in Paris on November 30th'; 'The YHA in Salzburg is neat'.

So it was. Salzburg is beautiful. The River Salzach winds its way through a town full of churches, cathedrals and abbeys and is dominated by the Festung Hohensalzburg, a huge fortress built on the heights above the town.

Allan and I had been out the night before with a group of travellers including people I had met in Berlin and the Czech Republic. It was getting colder – coming back from the pub in the early hours of the morning, we had to virtually skate over the bridge. We were up relatively early and set off for the Mozart Wohnhaus (Mozart's residence) down in the market square. Wolfgang Amadeus Mozart had lived and worked here from 1773 to 1787 and today it is a small museum of instruments, pictures and artefacts. It is a good museum, but it has no soul.

After a late lunch, we went up to the fortress. If you have the money you can travel part of the way up by cable car, but we climbed through impressive gate-houses, and past frost-encrusted daisies. As we went along, the fog started to drift in from the river, making the cobblestones slippery with dew. By the time we reached the top, the town was fading into the mist.

On the other side of the battlement we could still see the Alps, but as we wandered through the fortress, even these disappeared into cloud.

On the highest floor, a curator opened one of the windows, so we leant out, peering into the dusk. Everything was still and silent and covered in a blanket of white. The fortress walls seemed to disappear into an abyss – Salzburg was hidden below the cloud and mist.

Then up through the gloom we heard a flautist playing Mozart, the phrases rising and falling through the fog.

Magic, magic, magic.